Historic Visits
to
Mull, Iona
and
Staffa

Eve Eckstein

Historic Visitors to Mull, Iona and Staffa

by

Eve Eckstein

Excalibur Press of London
13 Knightsbridge Green London SW1X 7QL

Copyright © 1992 Eve Eckstein

Printed and bound in U.K.
Typesetting and origination by CBS Felixstowe Suffolk
Published by Excalibur Press of London
ISBN 1 85634 176 3

Contents

		Page
Introduction		
The Builders of Brochs and Standing Stones	4000-1500 BC	1
Ptolemy	146 AD	5
St. Columba	563	7
The Gravestone Carvers of Iona	c600-1560	9
Sir Donald Monro	1549	13
Johannes Blaeu	1596-1673	16
Martin Martin	1695	18
William Sacheverell	1702	22
Thomas Pennant	1771	30
Sir Joseph Banks	1772	36
Dr. Johnson	1773	40
James Boswell	1773	49
Faujas de St. Fond	1784	58
John Knox	1786	65
Thomas Campbell	1795	69
Dr. T. Garnett	1798	76
Dr. John Leyden	1800	85
Mrs. Murray	1800	92
Dorothy Wordsworth	1803	104
Sir Walter Scott	1810/1814	106
William Daniell	1815	111
Sir Charles Lyell	1817	114
John Keats	1818	119
John Macculloch	1824	125
Felix Mendelssohn	1829	128
William M. Turner	1831	132

William Wordsworth	1833	135
Sir Robert Peel	1837	139
John Wilson	1841	141
Statistical Survey of Argyll	1843	145
Tobermory		152
Queen Victoria	1847	155
Alfred Lord Tennyson	1853	158
Jules Verne	1859	161
William Black	1879	165
Robert Louis Stevenson	1885	
		169
Angela du Maurier	1937/1950	175
The Mitford Family	1930/1940s	180
Summary		184

List of Photographs and Illustrations

	Page
A Print of a so-called Danish Fort	4
A Reproduction of Ptolemy's Map	6
Selection of Carved Gravestones	12
A Map of the Hebrides	15
A Map of Mull by J Blaeu	17
A Print of Aros Castle in Ruins	28
The Tombs of the MacLeans, Iona	29
Thomas Pennant	34
Enlarged Print of Fingal's Cave	35
Early Print of Fingal's Cave	39
A Print of the Ruined Abbey of Iona	48
A Map Showing Dr Johnson's and Boswell's Travels	57
A Portrait of Faujas de St. Fond	63
The Interior of Fingal's Cave	64
The Entrance to the Harbour at Oban	68
A 19th. Century Print of the Interior of Fingal's Cave	75
Gylen Castle	84
Booshala, or The Herdsman, from the Cliff above	88
A Romantic View of Dunstaffnage Castle	91
View of the Summit of Staffa	101
Dramatic View of the Carsaig Arches	102
Map of Mull, Coll, Tyree, Iona, Staffa and the Treshnish Isles	103
A Print of the Sound of Mull	105
Mingary Castle	109
Torloisk House	110

A Print of Iona from the North East	113
Clamshell Cove	118
Passengers Being Ferried Across the Sound to Mull	123
Map of Keats' Tour of Mull	124
Sheet of Music Showing Part of Mendelssohn's "Hebridean Overture"	130
A German Engraving of Fingal's Cave	131
A Sketch of Turner's Vignette of the Interior of Fingal's Cave	134
The Summit of the Isle of Staffa	138
A French Print of Staffa	140
A View of the Clamshell Cove on Staffa	144
A Panoramic View of the Main Street of Tobermory	154
The Landing Place on Iona	157
A Print of the Interior of Fingal's Cave	160
Oban Harbour	164
An Interior View of the Ruined Abbey at Iona	168
The Dhu Heartach Lighthouse	173
Map Showing the Probable Course of David Balfour's Wanderings	174
Torosay Castle	179
View of Oban in the 1920s	183

Introduction.

The following collection of historical, literary and artistic reports from a wide variety of visitors to the Hebridean Islands of Mull, Iona and Staffa, from times as early as the 6th century and progressing through the years up until the 1950s, has been arranged in chronological order in the hope that it will give present day travellers and visitors a greater overall view of the development of the isles, and the considerable effects that these magical islands have had on famous people through the ages.

Today the visitor can still find that same peace and quiet for mind and body, enjoy the timeless quality which abounds, and receive quiet courtesy from the islanders. In fact, if you don't buy a newspaper or listen to the radio, it is very easy to forget the exact day of the week, just as the poet Thomas Campbell did in 1795.

In some ways the landscape has changed over the years. Dr. Johnson bemoaned the lack of trees in Mull in 1773; this was due to a great extent to the large population at the time, who tended to burn or use every piece of available wood which they could find. It was also accelerated in the 19th century by the large number of sheep, which tended to graze the hills so closely that few trees survived. These sheep led in time to the Clearances, when the people themselves and not just the trees were swept away. Now the number of sheep has been reduced and the trees flourish again in certain areas. Some forward-looking landowners began growing plantations of mixed trees during the 19th century; notable amongst these was Mrs. Clephane Maclean of Torloisk. On the whole, the landscape remains much as it has been for many generations, and the remains of the 'lazy beds' in which potatoes were grown can still be seen all over the islands. There is less land under the plough than fifty years ago, but this too is changing as certain 'incomers' realize the potential of the very fertile soil of Mull. (Iona has always been agriculturally advanced since St. Columba's time.)

By placing these excerpts chronologically, I hope today's visitors will get a greater idea of the continuity of events through successive reports on such items as the gradual disappearance of the marble altar on Iona, which is mentioned by several visiting historians (vandalism existed in the 18th century, even if it went under the different name of 'talisman hunting'); or the eventual understanding of how the basalt columns of Staffa were formed.

Keats and Wordsworth deplored the commercialism and the exploitation of the islands of Iona and Staffa, which may seem strange to us 200 years later; but who can predict the changes which will occur within the next 200 years?

The magical qualities of the islands have affected many people, from the Broch Builders and the erectors of Standing Stones in the very early years, through the period of map-makers, adventurous travellers, artists, poets, story-tellers and statistical surveyers to Royal visitors. All have made some statement, report, or have felt moved to sketch what they saw, or use the dramatic scenery as background for their novels. Some may seem today to be extremely romantic in their views, some patronizing to the islanders, whose way of life was very different to that of most of the visitors; but they are all typical of the times from which they 'speak', and so taken together I hope that these reports help to give a picture through the ages of the wonderful inspiration which has been produced by Mull, Iona and Staffa.

The Builders of Brochs, Duns and Standing Stones.

During the phase of British Pre-history which spans the time from 4000B.C. - 1500B.C, also known as the Earlier and Later (New Stone Age) period and the Early Bronze Age, early man began to settle down to become farmers, clearing tracts of forest in order to plant cereals.

The very large number of Brochs, Duns, Standing Stones and Stone Circles, on the Western coasts of the Inner and Outer Hebrides and on the West coast of the mainland, has led Professor Thom in his book Megalithic Sites in Britain to deduce that they were used in Megalithic Astronomy.

Astronomical observations were made from the positions of the circles and single stones. As described in John Ewin Wood's book Sun Moon and Standing Stones, Professor Thom accounted for the large number of lunar observations he had discovered particularly in Western Scotland. "As the technique (of lunar observations) improved, they became simpler and more effective. They were refined to the point where they consisted of a few carefully-positioned standing stones, often indicating a notch on the distant horizon. In this way, the techniques the men of the Early Bronze Age had been forced to invent in order to fix the exact date of the Solstices (the two times of the year midway between the two equinoxes, 20th March and 22nd Sept, when the sun, having reached the tropical points, is farthest from the equator and appears to stand still - about June 21st and December 22nd) were adapted to lunar observations and led finally to the construction of intricate devices for calculating eclipse phenomena, like the standing stones at Carnac and Kermario."

The theory was that eclipses could be predicted by moving

one stone to the right each night so that the standing stones and the notch in the distance were in alignment, and marking each position moved as one move. J.E. Wood says, "If we were to repeat this every month we should find that the monthly maximum markers advanced to the right and returned to the left. The furthest right of the monthly markers would give us the maximum of the minor perturbation (period when eclipses most likely to occur).... Since the minor perturbation has a period of 173 days it would have been possible to predict ahead and to know when the future eclipse danger period would occur." This may all sound very involved but it was of great importance to Neolithic and Early Bronze Age man to have an accurate calendar and the ability to predict eclipses obviously added greatly to the power and prestige of the priestly learned men, predecessors of the Druids.

Earthly Neolithic men were farmers and a reliable calendar was therefore necessary. In the period 1700BC onwards, a change in the weather conditions seem to have lessened astronomical activity. J.T. Woods records that "no stellar or lunar observations have been dated as late as 1600 BC.... The increased cloudiness would have hampered the observations, ultimately making it impossible to continue precise measurements....concurrently the crops would have begun to fail, the uplands would have become less and less habitable, and pressures for survival would have left little time for inessentials. Indeed, there are signs that many people did not survive, because the Early Bronze Age pottery types, beakers, urns etc, all disappear from later excavation layers."

According to Euan W. Mackie, editor of the <u>Glasgow Archaeological Journal 1980</u>, megalithic mathematics lingered on in Northern Scotland until the Iron Age. He studied the dimensions of the brochs. These remains are peculiar to Scotland. They are essentially hollow round towers of drystone walling, which may be up to 13m. high. The walls themselves are hollow and contain rooms and staircases. He applied statistical analysis to the diameter of the brochs and found them to be similar and based on a megalithic yard of 0.829m. "In view of the long lapse and changing cultures it is rather surprising that any trace of megalithic geometry should remain, but the similarity is too great to be accidental. We can only presume that a verbal tradition of some shapes being of some significance lingered on for fifteen centuries or more."

A print of a so-called Danish Fort, published in the 18th century, when it was supposed that these Duns and Brochs had been constructed by the invading Danes in the distant past.

Ptolemy. Egyptian Geographer A.D.146.

Early names for the Hebrides vary, but as some of these are very far back in historical time, this is not surprising.

Ptolemy, the mathematician, geographer and astronomer, who was one of the first to mention the Hebridean Islands, said, in the introduction to his geography, that: "Above Ireland are the isles called Eboudae five in number' and further west of Ebouda are other islands 'Rhicina, Malois and Epidiou'.

The word 'Hebouda' first appeared in the writings of Pliny, A.D.23-79, and he mentioned that there were over 30 'Hebudae' isles.

Adamnam describes Mull as ' Malea Insula' in his **Life of St. Columba**.

It is thought that the strange tilt to the east, which Ptolemy gave to Scotland (Thule) in his Geography, was due to the joining together of the two parts of the map of Scotland, in order to get them to fit onto one page. In the facsimile of Ptolemy's map which was published in May 1847 by A. and C. Black, Edinburgh, there are different spellings for Rhicina (Itiema), Malois (Maleos), and Epidiou (Epidium), which may have been the result of inaccurate copying.

The reproduction of Ptolemy's map
published by A and C. Black of Edinburgh in 1847.

St. Columba 563.

Most people probably know the story of St. Columba leaving Ireland in order to spread the news of Christianity and, landing first on Oronsay but finding that he could still see Ireland on the horizon, he re-embarked and sailed further North and landed on Iona. Here, having satisfied himself that he could no longer see his beloved homeland, he buried his coracle in the sand of the beach. He could see that Iona was an extremely fertile island. That, combined with its remoteness and its position, geographically close to the Picts but not part of the mainland of Scotland, suited his purpose ideally. Thomas Pennant in his book Tour of the Western Isles written in 1769 said that "St. Columba was soon distinguished by the sanctity of his manner and a miracle that he wrought, so operating on the Pictish King Bradeus that he immediately made a present of the little isle of Iona to the Saint. It seems his majesty had refused Columba an audience and even proceeded so far as to order the palace gates to be shut against him, but the Saint, by the power of the word, instantly caused them to fly open."

The twelve original followers of Columba were joined by other pioneers from Ireland, and they were soon all engaged in building, cultivating and organizing the Community. Their days were filled with "prayer, study and manual labour", according to F.M. M'Neill in his book on Iona: A History of the Island 1920. Columba was always ready to take his share of the physical labour. They were not recluses and the Columban Church was devoted to missionary work. They travelled first towards Inverness up the Great Glen, later to the Forth and Clyde areas.

Columba and his followers were skilled sailors, and Adamnan

(Columba's early biographer) mentions various types of boat which they used, coracles of wicker and hide, skiffs, barks, cobbles, freight ships and a longboat hollowed out of a single oak or pine trunk. The most adventurous of these sailor-monks was Cormac, who sailed as far north as Shetland and Orkney and probably to the Faroes and Iceland.

The Gravestone Carvers of Iona

There are many fascinating carved stones in the Relig Odhrain on Iona. These carved stones cover a wide period but can be divided into two main groups, Early Christian and medieval.

Early Christian

Beginning with the period of St. Columba's arrival in 563 and ending in the 12th century when the Celtic Monastery was replaced by a Benedictine Abbey.

The earliest stones which may date from the 7th century are roughly trimmed and have simple incised crosses. The ringed crosses with projecting arms beyond the circumference of the ring, which was common on Iona were a later development.

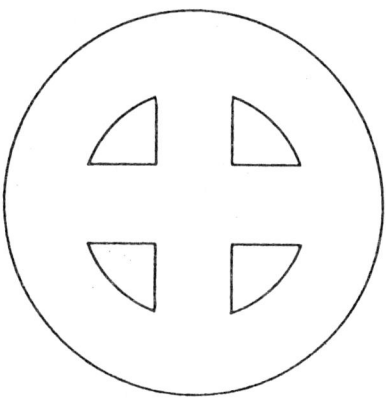

Incised cross. 7th century.

Occasional Viking raids in the late 8th and 9th centuries led to Iona coming under Norse influence from the end of the 9th century to the middle of the 12th century.

This influence is shown in two stones where the Norse runes read "Kili, son of Olive, placed this stone over his brother Fugl". The other shows a ship with six figures and a larger figure with a hammer and tongs forging a sword, which may have a connection with the story of Sigurd.

At the end of this Early Christian period we see a stage in the transition from crosses, where the interspaces between the cross and ring are completely pierced through, to those of the solid disc-headed crosses popular in the late medieval times.

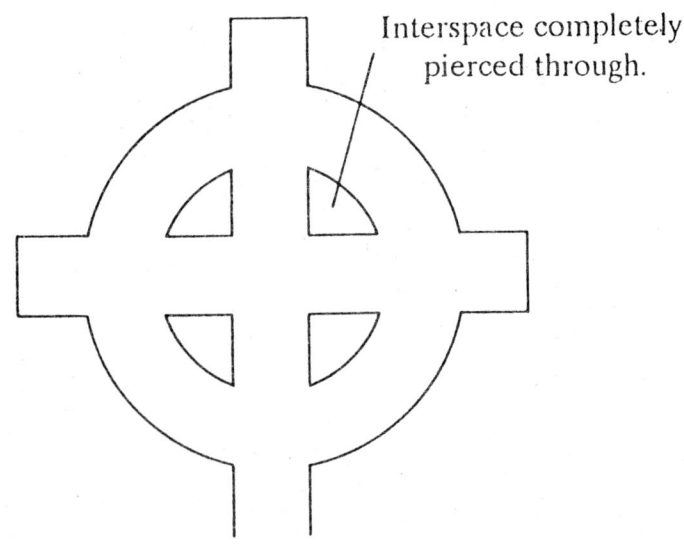

8th - 9th century.

Medieval

By the beginning of the 14th century a school of carving was established on Iona turning out a distinctive series of richly-decorated grave slabs and free-standing crosses, made at first just for island use. They were later exported to other parts of the Lordship of the Isles. The Iona School ceased production at the Reformation in 1560.

Much more elaborate than in the former period, these grave-slabs showed plant-scrolls, animals, abbots in mitres, hunting scenes, West Highland galleys, a Prioress with her lap dogs and a mirror and a comb, symbols of femininity.

References to these gravestones will be made by Thomas Pennant, T. Garnett, Dr. Johnson, Boswell and Wordsworth.

Further information on the carved stones can be found in the Iona Abbey bookshop.

Medieval Stylized West Highland Galley.

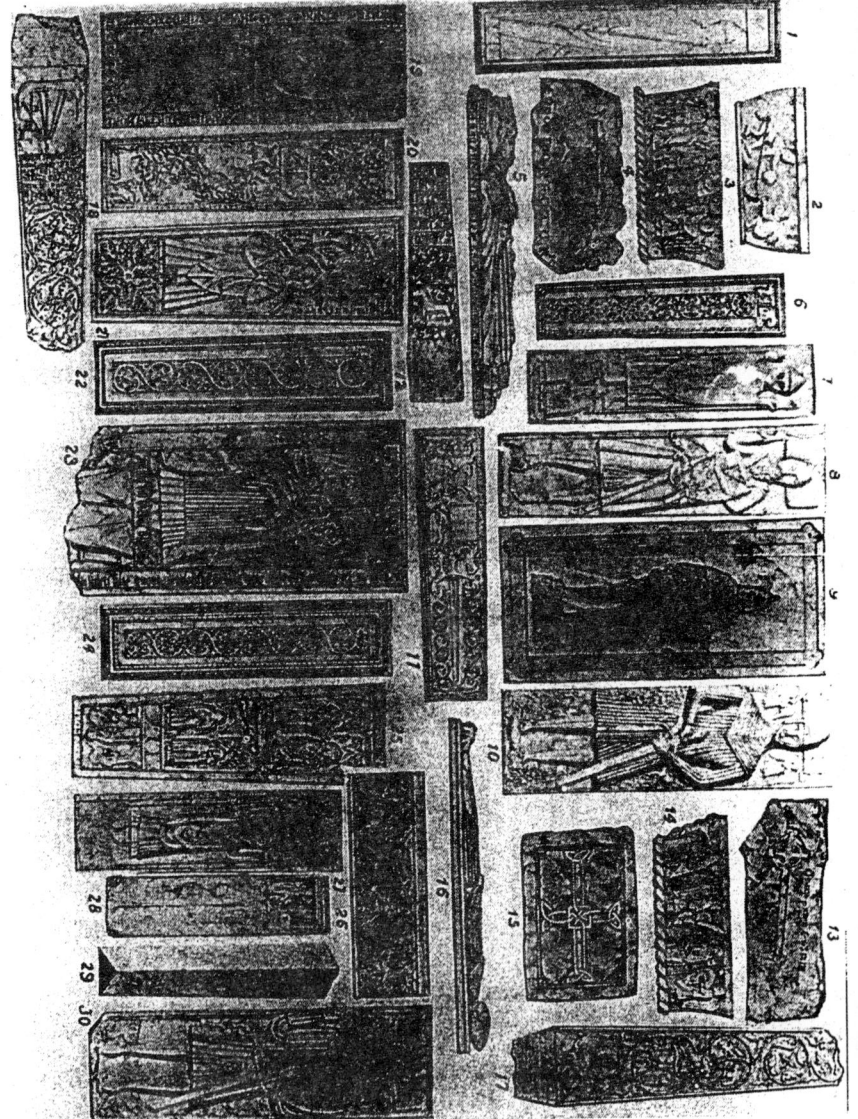

Selection of carved gravestones, showing figures of Churchmen and Prioresses, soldiers with long swords, ships, animals and a wide variety of Celtic decorative intertwining designs.

Sir Donald Monro, High Dean of the Isles.

Description of the Western Isles of Scotland called Hebrides, 1549.

Sir Donald Monro was born at the beginning of the 16th century and was related to several of the most influential families in the Highlands and Islands, including the Macleods of Lewis, so he had had an early association with the Western Isles.

Scotland was at the time passing through almost a century of disturbance. In 1526 Donald was presented to the Vicarage of Snizort in Raasay. The Bishopric of the Isles was the poorest and the most scattered, comprising as it did all the Islands off the western coast. As Monro himself said of the Abbey of Icolmkill or Iona, which was the Cathedral Church of the Bishop of the Isles, the Bishop's Palace on Iona was in ruins, it consisted of "a large hall open to the roof, a chamber, which I suppose he used a ladder to get into, and under the chamber, a buttery."

"The title 'High Dean of the Isles', which he added to his name, may have had little significance, but he styled himself Sir Donald, merely because that was the usual description in those days for a priest who had *not* studied at a University or obtained a degree." (From an unpublished m.s. and introductory notes by R.W. Munro).

He probably became Archdeacon when Roderick Maclean became Bishop to the Isles 1549-1555. One of his first acts was to make himself familiar with his Diocese, so he travelled through many of the Islands in 1549 as the 'Bishop's Eye'. He clung to his title of High Dean of the Isles even after the Reformation in

1560; he signed two Charters regarding the exchange of lands, styling himself as Dean of the Isles.

Sir Donald's description of Mull, although brief, gives a picture of the wild-life and landowners,

"Mull-Twelfe Myle northward from the Iyle of Colnansay lyes the Iyle of Mull, ane grate rough ile, noch the less it is fertile. This ile contains in length from the nortiest to the southweste 24 myles and in breid from eist southweste to west north west uther 24 myles with certain woodes, maney deire, and verey fair hunting games (with many grate mertines and cunnings for hunting with a guid raid fornent Comkill callit Pollaisse). There are sevin paroche kirks within this iyle and three castles, to wit the castle of Dowart (Duart), a strenthey place, bigged on a craige at the seaside, the castle of Lochbowy, pertaining to McGillayne of Lochbowy, the castle of Arose qullick in former times pertinct to the Lord of the Iyles and now is bruked by McGillayne of Dowart.... In this Ile there are two guid freshe waters, ane of them called Ananva and the waters of Glenforsay full of salmond with uther waters that has salmond in them byt not in sic aboundance as the two forsaid."

A translation of the part within the parentheses probably reads as follows: "...with many great martens (pinemartens) and rabbits (from cunnings/coneys) for hunting with a good road towards Icolmkill (Iona)."

Monro also gives us a rather different picture of Gometra describing it as "fruitful in proportion to the other isles" and also tells us that on the Calve island there is "a coppice, and affords good pasturage for all kinds of cattle. Between this isle and the isle of Mull, there is a capacious and excellent bay, called Toubir Mory (the Virgin Mary's well), because the water of that name, which is said to be medicinal, runs into the bay."

A map of the Hebrides published in the 16th century, and showing the Outer Hebrides and the Inner Hebrides as well as the whole of the Western part of Scotland in an unusual horizontal position.

Johannes Blaeu 1596-1673

The maps of both Johannes Blaeu and his father, William Janszoon Blaeu, were based on surveys made at least 35 years earlier by Timothy Pont. In the case of the map of Mull, which was probably published in 1647, it is based on Pont's survey carried out around 1600. Both the Blaeus admitted their indebtedness to earlier cartographers; the atlases which they produced were a very comprehensive survey of the world at that time.

Timothy Pont carried out a survey of Scotland between 1583-1601. This was comparable to those of the well-known mapmaker Saxton. Pont "travelled on foot right through the whole of this kingdom, as no-one before him had done." But he was unable to find a publisher for these Scottish maps. On his death about 1610 his manuscripts and maps passed into the possession of Sir James Balfour and were edited and revised by Robert Gordon of Straloch; and in 1654 Johannes Blaeu published them as Volume V of his Atlas Nova. This included 2 maps of Scotland, one Ancient Scotland and one modern Scotland, plus 46 maps covering all the different districts.

A map of Mull by J. Blaeu 1645.

Martin Martin

Description of the Western Isles of Scotland 1695.

Martin Martin's ancestral home was at Bealach in Skye. He was a tutor to Macdonald of Sleat and to the young laird, Macleod of Skye. He reported on the 17th century social customs in Mull, which at the time was an extremely fertile island, in sharp contrast to the later effects that overpopulation, famine and sheep had on the land during the 18th and 19th centuries.

"The isle is in the Sheffif-dom of Argyle and the air here is temperately cold and moist. The fresh breezes that blow from the mountains do in some measure qualify it. The natives are accustomed to take large doses of *aqua vitae* as a corrective when the season is very moist and then they are careful to chew a piece of charmel root, finding it to be aromatic, especially when they intend to have a drinking bout, for they say this in some measure prevents drunkenness.

"The mould (earth) is generally black and brown both in hills and valleys....the heath affords an abundance of turf and peats which serve the natives for good fuel. There is a great ridge of mountains about the middle of the island. One of them is very high, therefore it is called Ben Vore (Great Mountain). It is to be seen from all the Western Isles and a considerable part of the continent. Both the mountains and valleys afford good pasturage for all sorts of cattle as sheep, goats and deer, which herd among the hills and bushes. The horses are of low size yet very sprightly and their black cattle are likewise low in size but their flesh is very delicious and fine. There is an abundance of wild fowl in hills and valleys, among them blackcock, heath-hen, ptarmigan and very fine hawks: the seacoast affords all such fowl which are to be had in Western Isles.

"The corn growing here is only barley and oats. There is a great variety of plants; but no wood here except a few coppices on the coast. There are bays and places for anchorage about the isle....

"The black and white Indian nuts are found on the West side of the isle (washed up on the shore). The natives pulverize the black nut and drink it in boiling water to cure diarrhoea." (These nuts can still be found today washed across the Atlantic from the West Indies and they still are considered to be lucky.)

"There are several rivers that afford salmon and some rivers abound with black mussel that breeds pearls. Fresh water lakes have trout and eels: the whole isle is well watered with springs and fountains. They told me of a spring on the South side of Ben Vore that has yellow coloured stone at the bottom, which does not burn or become hot though it should be kept in a fire the whole day. Amphibia, seals, otters, vipers, foxes abound and do much hurt among the lambs and kids." (Foxes no longer exist on Mull)

"There are some forts called Dunns supposed to have been built by the Danes. They are round in form and have a passage all round within the walls. The door of them is low and many of the stones are of such bulk that no number of the present inhabitants could raise them without any engine. All stand on eminences and are in full view of one another so that a beacon in any one fort can communicate to all the rest and this has always been observed upon sight of any foreign vessels approach."

(I.F. Grant in **Highland Folkways** identifies Carmile (Charmel) as a tuberous bitter vetch (Lathyrus Macorrhizus) which he says "has been well known since ancient times for the property of preventing hunger on long journeys."

The West Indian nuts are from the plant *Entada Scandens*. It was believed that if held in the hand by a woman during labour it would ease the birthpains and also ward off evil fairies. During the 18th and 19th centuries the nuts were mounted in silver and hung from watch-chains.

Lathyrus Macorrhizus

William Sacheverell

An account of the journey to The Isle of Man & a Voyage to I-colmkill (Iona) in 1688. Published 1702.

William Sacheverell was involved in Parliamentary affairs from 1607-1691 and was also M.P. for Northampton. He was extremely interested in attempting to recover the lost treasure from the Spanish galleon which, when the Spanish Armada was scuttled in 1588 and escaped around the north and west coast of Scotland, took shelter in Tobermory harbour. Her captain, Don Pereira, had had an argument regarding payment for refitting and supplying her with stores, with Sir Lachlan Mor Maclean of Duart. They each took two hostages from their followers and tradition has it that when Pereira attempted to sail away without paying, one of his Scottish hostages managed to set fire to the galleon's magazine, blowing himself and the ship to pieces. One of the famous medical family of Beatons from Pennygael was sitting on the deck at the time, but fortunately he was blown clear and landed in the harbour unharmed. The galleon was supposed to be carrying a cargo of 30 million Ducats and some Church plate of immense value, and this has led to many unsuccessful attempts to salvage the galleon, Sacheverell's being one of the earliest.*

In the summer of 1688 Sacheverell and his divers "saluted the Castle of Duart with 5 guns" as they sailed up the Sound of Mull arriving at 'Tauber Murry' in the evening. Sacheverell was impressed by the setting where "3 or 4 Cascades of Water, which throw themselves from the Top of the Mountain, with a pleasure that is astonishing....the Mountains and woods are pleasantly mixed with Rocks....which make one oddest and most charming Prospects I ever saw. Italy herself, with all its Assistance of Art can hardly afford anything more Beautiful and Diverting."

During the first week of his visit, "The weather was pleasant, but spent in fitting our (Diving) Engines, which Prov'd very well, and every way suited our design: and our Divers outdid all Examples of this Nature: But with the Dog-days, the Autumnal Rains usually begin in these parts, and for six weeks we had scarce a good day. The whole Frame of Nature seem'd inhospitable, black, Stormy, Rainy, Windy, so that our Divers could not bear the cold."

He had previously watched other divers "especially when the weather was clear and serene....sinking threescore Foot under Water, and stay sometimes above an hour and at last returning with the spoils of the Ocean; whether it were Plate or Money, it convinced us of the Riches and Splendour of the once thought invincible Armada."

Because of the continuing bad weather Sacheverell set off across Mull on Aug. 23rd in order to reach Iona. The country he encountered was like a "wild desert," the men he observed to be "large Bodied, Stout, Subtile, Active, Patient of Cold and Hunger: there appeared in their Actions a certain generous air of freedom, and contempt of those trifles, Luxury and Ambition, which we so servily creep after. Tho' their habits were mean, and they had not our sort of Breeding, yet in many of them there was a Natural Beauty, and a graceful Modesty, which never fails of Attraction. The usual outward Habit of both Sexes is the Plaid, the Womens much finer, the Colours more lively and the squares larger than the Men's....this serves them for a Veil, and covers both head and body. The Men wear theirs after another manner, especially when design'd for Ornament; it is loose and flowing, like the Mantles our Painters give their heroes. Their thighs are bare, with brawny Muscles; Nature has drawn all her Strokes bold and Masterly. What is cover'd, is only adapted to necessity, a thin Brogue on the Foot, a short Buskin of various colours on the Legg, tied above the Calf with a strip'd pair of Garters. What should be conceal'd is hid with a large Shot-pouch, on each side of which hangs a Pistol, and a Dagger; as if they found it necessary to keep those parts well guarded. A round Target (shield) on their backs, a blew (blue) Bonnet on their Heads, in one Hand a broad Sword, and a Musquet in the other which they will handle with bravery and dexterity, especially in the Sword and Target."

Aug. 24th. The journey after breakfast with the Earl of Argyll's Bailiff near Aros Castle, was rough, "over a country broken, rocky, boggy, barren, and almost wholly unarable. Besides, the weather was very unseasonable, so that tho' our whole day's Journey was but 16 Miles it seemed at least Six and Twenty. But wet and weary at last we came to a Change House (so they call a House of Entertainment) if a place that had neither Bed, Victuals or Drink, may be allow'd that name. Our servants cut us green fern (wet as it was) for Bedding....if I thought the first day's Journey hard and unequal, this was much worse; high craggy Mountains, horrid Rocks and dreadful Precipieces. However After 10 Miles riding we came to the further Shoar: with great difficulty we procur'd a boat, and had then 3 Leagues to row thro' Rocks. on which we struck several times." They landed safely on Iona and Sacheverell spoke of a two storey building, and of a Library being still recognisable. The remains of "Cloyster behind the Church, which leads to several Appartments; as likewise of a Library, as we suppose, and under it a large room, which they told us was for Public Disputations; some good lodgings, which we thought were the Abbots'.... I had the Curiousity to measure the Church; the Choir was 20 yds long, the Cupulo 21 Foot Square, the body of the Church the same length with the Choir, and the Cross-Isles half that length. On each side of the Choir are two little Chapels, the entrance to them opening with large Pillars curiously carv'd in Basso Relievo; the Steeple was lofty, tho' I had not opportunity to take the just height nor that of the Church. There was formerly a fine Ring of Bells, which have been sold.''

He was able to decipher, what must have been one of the Grave slabs of the "latter Abbots, whom I found by the inscription to be of the noble Family of the Mac-Kenning, or Mac-Kenzy. A Statue is of black Marble curiously wrought, as big as the Life, in an Episcopal Habit, with a Mitre, Crozier Ring....and in the middle of a flat stone a Man in Armour engrav'd, which seems very ancient.''

Temptingly, he mentions a book which a Mr. John Frazer, Dean of the Isles told him of. His father who had also been Dean of the Isles, had left him a book with more than 300 hundred inscriptions but he had lent it to the late Earl of Argyll, "a man of incomplete sense and great curiousity, and doubts they are all lost by the great man's afflictions." One wonders if they will ever be found.

Another interesting point which Sacheverell mentions is that of the "Ancient Altar of the Church, one of the finest pieces of white Marble I ever saw. It is about 6 foot long, and 4 broad, curiously vein'd and polish'd, it is all yet entire, except one corner which has been broke by accident.'' Dr. Johnson, 85 years later in 1773, mentioned the destruction of this altar by those who sought a talisman to safeguard them against being shipwrecked.

Sacheverell was interested in wildlife and made enquiries about the local Fowls and Animals. "I was particularly curious concerning the Barnacle or Anser Abietanus. They are all Positive that there is nothing more frequent than to have large branches of fir, thrown upon these Western Islands with shells growing on them in which the Foetus is enclosed, when they are to be seen with Bills, Wings, Legs, Feathers, and everything previous to life.... A devine I since met with assured me has seen them have actual Motions, and another (of great worth) that upon keeping them out of the water, they will in a few days putrify and smell intolerably." This must be a description of the Acorn Barnacle, which does indeed "have actual Motions" when kept out of water. It is in appearance very similar to a fir tree branch, so perhaps it isn't surprising that its description caused confusion as to whether it was a bird or a shell, or even a plant.

The Goose Barnacle is the name given to a ship barnacle (Lepas) or the common acorn barnacle (Balnus) which consists of a long fleshy stalk, attaching the animal to floating wood, and a series of five white calcareous shells at the end of the stalk, which enclose six pairs of branched appendages (Cirri). By means of these cirri the animal filters from the water minute particles on which it feeds. (Description from the Encyclopaedia Britannica)

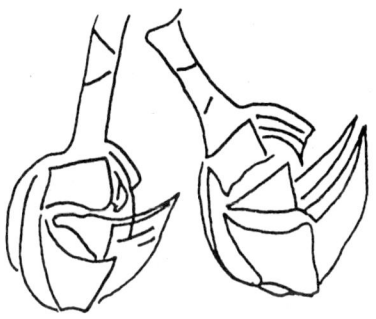

*Recent research into the Tobermory Galleon has resulted in the probability that there was little or no actual treasure on board. Full details of this research can be found in the excellent Mull Museum in Tobermory, which has displays of various historical items and photographs of the many standing stones on the island as well as old prints and maps.

A print of Aros castle in 'ruins from the 19th century', showing the Castle in its prominent position overlooking the Sound of Mull. Aros was often used as a landing place for travellers from the mainland of Scotland.

The tombs of the Macleans buried on the Isle of Iona. (These historic gravestones are now on view in the Museum behind the Abbey, where they can be protected from the elements). This photograph was taken in the early 20th century.

Thomas Pennant's Voyage 1771

Thomas Pennant made two tours to the western Isles in 1771 and a second the following year. He travelled on horseback and was accompanied by the Ref. J. Lightfoot, the botanist, and author of Flora Scotia published in 1777.

From Pennant's elaborate journal we learn that he visited Iona in July before arriving at Tobermory in August. While approaching Iona he noticed "multitudes of gannets fishing, plunging on their prey at least two fathoms deep and which took to the air again as soon as they emerged. Their sense of seeing must be exquisite; but they are often deceived, for Mr. Thompson informed me that he had frequently taken them by placing a herring on a hook and sinking it a fathom deep, which the gannet plunges for and thus is 'taken'." Gannets were eaten and their skin provided material for shoes. There is a recipe for cooking them in the modern Jubilee Cook Book of Mull published in 1977. "Wild geese breed here and are often reared and tamed by the natives."

"The view of Iona was very picturesque: the East side....exhibited a beautiful variety; an extent of plain, a little elevated above the water, and almost covered with the ruins of the sacred buildings, and the remains of the old town, still inhabited. Beyond these the island rises into little rocky hills with narrow verdant hollows between. ....The soil is a compound of sand seashells and black loam....it is in perpetual tillage....oats do not succeed here; but flax and potatoes come on very well." Pennant also commented on the wild flora: "The beautiful Sea-Bugloss makes the shores gay, with its glaucous leaves and purple flowers. The Eryngo or sea holly is frequent; and the fatal Belladonna is found here."

"The tennants here run-rig, and have the pasturage in common. It supports about a hundred-and-eight head of cattle and about five-hundred sheep."

Despite these observations Pennant found the inhabitants of Iona the "most stupid and most lazy of all the islanders; yet many of them boast of their descent from the company of St. Columba."

Like Dr. Johnson he reported that the floor of the Church attached to the nunnery was covered "some feet thick with cow dung, the place being at present the common shelter for cattle." "With much difficulty by virtue of fair words and a bribe," Pennant prevailed, "on one of these listless fellows to remove a great quantity of this dunghill" so that he could see the tomb of the last prioress. "Her figure is cut on the face of the stone, an angel on each supports her head and above there is a plate and a comb" (actually a mirror and a comb). This tombstone can be seen now amongst the carved gravestones in the museum. (See earlier comment on carved stones).

He also noticed that the gravestones in the *Reilig Ourain* or the burying place of Oran were "so overgrown with weeds, especially the common butter-burr, that very few are at present to be seen." On the road to the Bay of Martyrs "is a large cross, called that of Macleane, one of the three-hundred-and-sixty, that were standing in this island at the Reformation, but almost immediately after were almost entirely demolished by order of a provincial assembly, held on the island."

One of the most interesting references is to the Black Stones which seem to have had a particular significance at this time, being used for the swearing of oaths. Pennant located them "in a corner of the cloister of the monastery behind the cathedral, were some black stones held so sacred, but for what reason I am ignorant, that it was customary to swear by them." (See comments by Dr. Johnson and William Wordsworth.)

Pennant reported that he walked amongst the ruins. The Abbot's Mount over-looked the whole monastery. "Beneath seem to have been the gardens, once well cultivated, for we are told that the monks transplanted from other places herbs both escalient (for culinary use) and medicinal. Beyond the Mount are the ruins of a kiln and a granary, and near it a mill. The lake or pool that served it lay behind; it is now drained and is the turbery (a piece of land where peat may be cut for fuel)....they neglect at present the convenience of a mill and use only querns." (See Garnett's A Tour Through the Hebrides.)

But perhaps the most interesting observation he makes is related to the library, once attached to the cathedral. It was the repository for most of the current Scottish Records, Pennant says. "The library must have been invaluable, if we can depend on Boethius who asserts that Fergus II, assisting Alaric the Goth in the sacking of Rome, brought away as a share of the plunder a chest of books which he presented to the Monastery of Iona. A similar parcel was taken from Iona to Aberdeen in 1525 and great pains were later used to unfold them, but through age and tenderness of the parchment, little could be read." What modern techniques could have made of these historic documents hardly bears thinking about! The records and register of the island all written on parchment were all destroyed at the time of the Reformation.

Pennant visited Staffa which he found so impressive that he said, "The mind can hardly form an idea more magnificent than such a space, supported on each side by ranges of columns; and roofed by the bottoms of those which have been broke off in order to form it; between the angles of which a yellow stalagmitic matter has exuded, which serves to define the angles precisely."

After Staffa they travelled on to Tobermory where a piece of the wreck of the Spanish Galleon was given to him by an old inhabitant. On August 9th they left Tobermory at 8.0 am and by 10.30 am they anchored opposite Aros Castle where at the foot of the rock is the ruin of an oval pier to which he secured his boat while he breakfasted with Mr. Campbell of Aros.

Pennant's interest in livestock means he recorded that in the years around 1769 Mull exported 1800 head of cattle, which were sold for 30-50 shillings a piece.

He makes an interesting comment on the famous Beaton family gravestone: "The memory of this old doctor of Mull has had a better fate" (than the nameless Kings of France whose inscriptions have been worn away. The Beaton memorial is preserved in these words:

"Hic jacet Johannes Betonus Maclenorum familiae, medicus qui mortuus 19 Novembris 1657 AET 63 Donaldus Betonus fecit 1674."

Thomas Pennant

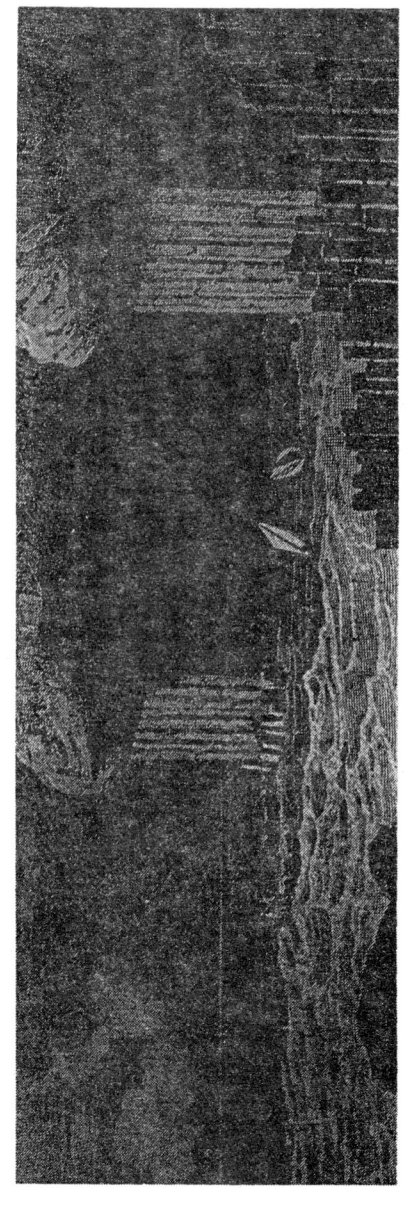

A much enlarged Fingal's Cave entrance with tiny boats sailing into it.

Sir Joseph Banks. Staffa visit 1772.

Sir Joseph Banks, president of the Royal Society 1778-1819, and famous naturalist, had visited Newfoundland in 1766, collecting plants. In 1768 he began the famous voyage with Captain Cook in which they made so many discoveries in the New World. On his return Banks planned a visit to Iceland and it was while starting this journey for the Natural History Society that, by very good fortune, he met a Mr. Leach from Ireland who was visiting Mr. Maclean of Drimnen in Morven on a fishing excursion; and while sailing close to Staffa he was so "struck by the singularity of its appearance, he landed upon it and examined it particularly." A few days later Sir Joseph Banks, on his way to Iceland cast anchor in the Sound of Mull, opposite to Drimnen and was immediately invited to land by Mr. Maclean, who entertained him and his party with great hospitality. Here Mr. Leach related to Banks what he had seen, "which excited his curiosity so strongly that he could not resist the offer made by this gentleman to accompany him to Staffa."

The account of this island drawn up by this celebrated naturalist was communicated to Mr. Pennant, who published it in his Tour in Scotland and a Voyage to the Hebrides; and this was the first description of the island ever presented to the public. It was accompanied by 6 engravings of Staffa. Banks felt that "the mind can hardly form an idea more magnificent than such a place, supported on each side by ranges of columns and roofed over by the bottom of those which have broken off from it, between the angles of which a yellow stalagmite matter has exuded which serves to define the angles precisely and at the same time vest the columns with a great deal of elegance and to render them still more agreeable. The whole is lighted from without so that the furthest extremity is very plainly seen from without." He also comments on the freshness of the cave, "the air, being agitated by the flux and reflux of the tides, is perfectly dry and wholesome, free entirely from the damp vapours with which natural caverns in general abound."

In his report in Vol.XXXVI (1772) of Scots Magazine he states that Staffa is "one of the greatest natural curiosities in the world, it is surrounded by many pillars of different shapes such as pentagons, octagons etc." In yet another report Banks declares that "compared to this (Staffa), what are the Cathedrals or the Palaces built by man? Mere models or playthings, imitations as diminutive as his works will always be compared with those of Nature. Where is the boast of the architect? Regularity, the only part in which he fancied himself to exceed his Mistress Nature, is here found in her possession, and here it has been for ages undiscovered."

Banks himself does not tell us of a very amusing incident which occurred during the night which they spent on the Island. It is recounted in the report by Faujas de St. Fond, the famous geologist, in his book Travels in England and Scotland Vol III. "On their arrival at Staffa they (Banks and his party) erected a tent....to pass the night, but the only inhabitant pressed Sir Joseph to come and sleep in his hut, and that out of compliance he consented and left his companions under the tent. On leaving the hut next morning he discovered he had acquired a colony of vermin. He mentioned the circumstances to his host in terms of mild surprise, but the latter, who was touched to the quick, perked himself up and, assuming a tone of consequence, reported haughtily and harshly that it was Sir Joseph himself who had imported the lice to his island and adding that it would have been better to have left them behind in England."

Donald MacCulloch in his book <u>Staffa</u> reports a recent discovery by Miss Barker of Cumberland of, the letters of J.B.1772 carved in a column at the very inner end of Fingal's cave; they are on a particularly difficult position to reach and it is considered unlikely to be the work of a hoaxer.

An early print of Fingal's Cave on Staffa, which owes a good deal to the imagination of the artist, and one wonders whether he was copying the work of another artist, and had never actually been to the Cave himself. Certainly the visitor standing on the columns is expressing great amazement at the wonder of Staffa.

Dr. Samuel Johnson 1773

When Dr. Johnson was nearing the end of his tour, he came to Mull from the isle of Coll with the Laird of Coll who had been such a wonderful guide to Johnson and Boswell. Their main destination was Iona, which Boswell had set his heart on visiting. So they arrived at Tobermorie in the middle of October 1773.

Oct 14th. The young Laird of Coll was "determined not to lose his company while there was any difficulty remaining....his influence soon appeared; for he procured us horses, conducted us to the house of Dr. Maclean, his uncle, where we found very kind entertainment and pleasing conversation," which was always sought after by Johnson; and he was particularly pleased to find that Miss Maclean, although "born in Glasgow, having removed with her father to Mull, added to other qualifications a great knowledge of the Earse language....gained by study of Earse poetry, that ever I could find."

Johnson described Mull as being "perhaps in extent the third of the Hebrides. It is not broken by waters, nor shot into promontories, but is a solid and compact mass, of breadth nearly equal to its length." Although he does say that of the "dimensions of the larger islands, there is no knowledge approaching exactness" he estimates fairly correctly that it contains "about three-hundred square miles." From his earlier comment about Mull not being broken by waters he cannot have seen the map made by Blaeu in 1647, although not very accurate, does show Mull to be "broken by waters and shot with promontories."

Oct 16th. After a day at Dr. Maclean's (this was Erray House which still stands on the outskirts of Tobermory) where Johnson "could have been well contented to stay longer....they pursued their journey. This was a day of inconvenience, as the country was very rough, and my horse was but little." Because of the barrenness of the countryside, Johnson reflects on "whether something may not be done to give Nature a more cheerful face, and whether those hills and moors that afford heath cannot with a little care and labour bear something better? The first thought that occurs is to cover them with trees." He could see stumps and roots in the ground. "But there is a frightful interval between the seed and the timber." He calculates that the growth of trees has the "unwelcome remembrance of the shortness of life, driven hard upon him." .... "Having not any experience of a journey on Mull, we had no doubt of reaching the sea by daylight and therefore we had not left Dr. Maclean's very early....we were always struggling with some obstruction or other, and our vexation was not balanced by any gratification of the eye or mind." A cross-country journey with no track can at any time be very exhausting. Johnson had been "long enough acquainted with hills and heath to have lost the emotion they once raised.... Under Col's protection we were sure of escaping all real evils. There was no house on Mull to which he could not introduce us." Unfortunately their next host, with whom they had planned to stay at a house on the coast "lay in bed without hope of life." (This must have been Torloisk House, often a setting-off point for Staffa or Iona, as will be seen later). They "resolved not to embarrass a family in a time of so much sorrow" and went on towards the Strait between Mull and Ulva.

They were assisted in their crossing to Ulva by the master of an Irish ship who "with great civility sent us his boat which quickly conveyed us to Ulva, where we were very liberally entertained by Mr. Macquarry" (whose son Col. Macquarie was to become Governor General of New South Wales from 1809-1821, and whose Mausoleum was built at Gruline.) Macquarry was the proprietor of Staffa as well as Ulva, and Johnson made a comment on a report that the Islanders were insensible to the wonders of Staffa. "They had indeed considered it little, because they had always seen it; and none but philosophers, nor they always are struck with wonder, otherwise than by novelty." Johnson also wanted to find out more about the ancient custom of *Mercheta Mulierum* which was still continued on Ulva, whereby a fine is due to the Laird at the marriage of one of his tenant's daughters. "This payment was, for want of money, made anciently in the produce of the land. Macquarry was used to demand a sheep for which he now takes a crown.... A sheep has always the same power of supplying human wants, but a crown will bring at one time more at another less." Johnson's comments are somewhat ambiguous, but Boswell's are more explicit.

Oct 17th. On reaching their next overnight staying place, on Inch Kenneth, Johnson and Boswell were once again very fortunate in their hosts. "Romance does not often exhibit a scene that strikes the imagination more than this little desert in the depth of western obscurity, occupied not by a gross herdman, or amphibious fisherman, but by a gentleman and two ladies of high birth, polished manners and elegant conversation, who in a habitation raised not very far above the ground, but furnished with unexpected neatness and convenience, practised all the kindness of hospitality, and the refinement of courtesy." What is more, Sir Allan, the Chieftain of the great clan of Maclean had "conveyed to his cottage a collection of books, and what else is necessary to make his home pleasant." They were reminded that it was Sunday which Sir Allan "never suffered to pass without some religious distinction, and invited us to partake in his act of domestick worship" which Johnson hopes "neither Mr. Boswell nor myself will be suspected of a disposition to refuse."

After looking for the ruins of an ecclesiastical library which neither he nor even Mr. Boswell, "who bends a keener eye on vacancy were able to perceive," they visited the Chapel and then "went with a boat to see the oysters in the bed, out of which the boatman forced up as many as were wanted."

Oct 18th. The next day they entreated Sir Allan to give them his protection and his company on the journey to Icolmkill. After a little hesitation he "promised to carry us on the morrow in his boat." In the evening one of the ladies played on her harpisicord, while Col and Mr. Boswell danced a Scottish Reel with the other. Again Johnson "could have easily been persuaded to a longer stay....but life will not be all passed in delight." Boswell had to be back in Edinburgh in time for the legal sessions. They took their "last embrace" of Col, that "amiable man" who, as Johnson says, "while these pages were preparing to attest to his virtues, perished in the passage between Ulva and Inch Kenneth." On such emotional matters Johnson is terse and factual; Boswell expresses his emotions more verbally.

Sir Allan landed them on the Mull coast in order to show them Mackinnon's Cave. They had forgotten to carry tapers; one little candle was produced and they managed to explore for the "eleventh part of a mile" and see the square stone called 'Fingal's Table'; but they feared to go further with their limited light, as had some "former adventurer....who was reported never to have returned." Johnson made the point that "no man should travel unprovided with instruments for taking heights and distances," nor should he fail to write down his findings at once. Having re-embarked, they passed by the headland of Atun (Ardtoun on Blaeu's map and known nowadays as The Wilderness). They saw columnar formations "not less worthy of curiosity than those of Staffa" as Sir Allan points out. Farther along the coast they stopped at more broken pilasters which "easily accommodated them with seats for refreshment." (See Blaeu's map)

The moon had risen by the time they passed the Nuns Island and arrived at "Icolmkill, and the islanders carried us over the water.... We were now treading that illustrious Island, which was once the luminary of the Caledonian regions, whence savage clans and roving barbarians derived the benefits of knowledge, and the blessings of religion. To abstract the mind from all local emotion would be impossible....whatever withdraws us from the power of our senses; whatever makes the past, the distant, or the future predominate over the present, advances us in the dignity of thinking beings.... That man is little to be envied, whose patriotism would not gain force upon the plain of Marathon, or where piety would not grow warmer among the ruins of Iona."

The headman "produced more provision than men, not luxurious, require. Our lodging was next to be provided. We found a barn well stocked with hay, and made our beds as soft as we could."

Oct 20th. Wed. Next morning they "rose and surveyed the place." Johnson took some measurements but said, "Mr. Pennant's delineations, which are doubtless exact, have made my unskilful description less necessary." The floor of the cathedral "is so incumbered with mud and rubbish, that we could make no discoveries of curious inscriptions....the place is said to be known whence the Black Stones lie concealed (see Pennant and Wordsworth) on which the old Highland Chiefs, when they made contracts and alliances, used to take the oath, which was considered as more sacred than any other obligation, and which could not be violated without the blackest infamy."

Like Pennant, Johnson also found the floor of the nunnery chapel "too miry for examination....so that some of the stones which covered the later Abbesses have inscriptions, which might yet be read if the chapel were cleaned." He also commented on the superstition that pieces of the marble altar in the nunnery were "a defence against shipwrecks, fire and miscarriages" so much so that it had been destroyed by the talisman seekers. He added more detail to Pennant's account of the life of St. Columba and his followers, saying, "The fishponds are yet discernible, and the aqueduct which supplied them is still in use."

Two of the houses on Iona at that time had chimneys but it is not used "for the farmers had made their fire....in the middle of the room....and they rejoiced, like their neighbours, in the comforts of smoke."

Oct 20th: Dr Johnson noted, "It is observed that ecclesiastical colleges are always in the most pleasant and fruitful places.... This island is remarkably fruitful" - despite seventy families living there - "yet both corn and cattle are annually exported." "The island, which was once the metropolis of learning and piety, has now no school for education nor temple for worship, only two of the inhabitants can speak English, and not one that can read or write." As they left, the islanders gathered round and pushed their boat down the beach, "every man....happy in the opportunity of being, for a moment, useful to his Chief (Sir Allan)." And Johnson foresees that "perhaps in the Revolutions of the world, Iona may be sometime again the instructress of the Western Regions." An interesting foresight, if one considers the impact of the Iona Community.

The night of the 20th was spent on Mull at the house of Mr. Maclean, "whose elegance of conversation and strength of judgement would make him conspicuous in places of greater celebrity." High praise indeed from Johnson. They travelled on next day "to the house of a very powerful Laird, Maclean of Lochbuy; for in this country every man's name is Maclean." He was "a true Highland Laird, rough and haughty, and tenacious of his dignity; who, hearing my name, inquired whether I was of the Johnstones of Glencoe, or of Ardnamurchan." Johnson doesn't tell us how he responded but Boswell records that Dr Johnson gave him a significant look, but made no answer; and "I told the Laird that he was not Johnstone but Johnson, and that he was an Englishman!"

Johnson ended his visit to the Hebrides with a discourse on Scottish castles which had been vacated by their owners for a more modern mansion nearby. This is particularly interesting at Lochbuy, because when Johnson and Boswell stayed there the Macleans had moved fairly recently into the then much more modern house, from the four-square castle complete with dungeon described by Johnson on the next page. This more modern house was only in use for about forty years before the Maclean family moved again into the classically designed rectangled house still in use today. The house Johnson stayed in stands behind the present house and is used for agricultural purposes.

Johnson ponders on the position of the castles in the Hebrides which are always (built) upon points of land, on the margin of the sea. He sees them of no use in days of piracy, nor as lighthouses, nor as places of retreat, feeling that the occupants could have been "suddenly surprised"; but seems to fail to grasp that the advantages of a sea look-out were all-important to the Lords of the Western Isles, enabling them to watch all sea traffic and any enemy arrivals. From the earliest days, forts and brochs had been built near the coast and were also within sight of each other, so that a beacon lit on one could quickly warn a whole island of an imminent attack. With roads or tracks so poor, most travelling was done by sea. So castles were much more likely to be built close to the coast.

Johnson gave a very detailed architectural description of Lochbuy Castle: "The single tower of three or four stories, of which the walls are sometimes eight or nine feet thick, with narrow windows, and close winding stairs of stone. The top rises in a cone or pyramid of stone, encompassed by battlements. Strongly fortified and almost impregnable....the only danger was at the gates, over which the wall was built with a square canopy....through this hollow the defendants let fall stones....and poured down water, perhaps scalding water.... In every castle is a well or dungeon." The well at Lochbuy is particularly interesting as the basin it fills keeps a constant level, never overflowing and never running dry. It is thought that there must be a type of S-bend system which keeps the water in the basin at a constant level. Johnson concludes by saying: "Of these islands it must be confessed that they have not many allurements, but to the mere lover of naked nature. The inhabitants are thin, provisions are scarce, and desolation and penury give little pleasure."

Boswell and Johnson "embarked in a boat" a few miles from Lochbuy, "in which the seat provided for our accommodation was a heap of rough brushwood; and on the twenty-second of October we reposed at a tolerable inn on the Mainland." Their tour of the Western Isles was over.

A print of the ruined Abbey of Iona made in the late 18th century, showing the remains of walls, on the left-hand side, which were once part of the domestic area of the 'Cathedral' as Johnson called it, the cattle can be seen in close proximity to the actual Abbey building, so it is not surprising that they should have taken shelter there in bad weather.

James Boswell 1773

James Boswell was a lawyer in Edinburgh, a friend of Dr. Johnson, who set himself to record all the conversations and ideas of Dr. Johnson. They travelled together on their tour of the Western Isles in 1773. Boswell's great desire was to visit Iona, whereas Dr. Johnson's was more to see for himself how life was lived in the remote parts of Scotland. Boswell's wife was not keen on her husband accompanying Dr Johnson, who she considered dissipated and said that, although she "had seen many a bear led by a man she had never before seen a man led by a bear." Boswell's Journal of the Tour of the Hebrides was not published until after the death of Johnson, because Johnson objected to it being published as an appendix of his own narrative, probably fearing the ridicule it was likely to invoke, so it appeared in 1786. Thomas Rowlandson, the satirical caricaturist, published a set of cartoons depicting the adventures which befell the two intrepid travellers.

From Boswell's account we learn a great deal of the background to the day-to-day events of their journey. Some items mentioned by Boswell which give us an insight into their relationship are not mentioned at all by Johnson so we are very indebted to Boswell, for it is the combination of the two accounts which makes the whole trip so complete and amusing.

Before reaching Coll and Mull their tour had taken in parts of the Highlands and visits to Skye and Raasay.

Oct. 14th 1773: they arrived in Mull, sailing into the harbour of Tobermory, and Boswell comments, "Dr. Johnson had owned to me that he was a good deal out of humour. Indeed, he showed it a good deal in the ship; for when I was expressing my joy....on landing in Mull, he said he had no joy, when he recollected that it would be five days before he could get to the Mainland. I was afraid he would now take a sudden resolution to give up seeing Icolmkill (Iona). A dish of tea and some good bread and butter....and his bad humour went off. They talked a good deal....and Col returned from his aunt....she insisted that we should come to her house." (Erray House, still standing on the outskirts of Tobermory)

"The Duke of Argyle's factor in Tyrie....a genteel agreeable man....was going to Inverary, and promised to put letters into the post-office for us. I now found that Dr. Johnson's desire to get to the mainland arose from his anxiety....to convey letters to his friends." These letters were indeed important to Johnson for no sooner had they supped than "he asked me to give him some paper to write letters. I begged he should write short ones....he was irritated by this and said, 'What must be done, must be done; the thing is past a joke'.... 'Nay Sir,' said I, 'write as much as you please;....You were very impatient this morning; but no sooner do you find yourself in good quarters, than you forget that you are to move.'"

Oct 15th. Friday arrived "a violent storm....and the rivers impassable"; this bad weather prevented them setting off, but when Boswell expressed discontent Johnson said, "Now that I have an opportunity of writing....I am in no such haste. I was amused with his being so easily satisfied; for the truth was that the gentleman who was to convey the letters....was not to set out for Inverary for some time; I did not undeceive my friend."

Oct 16th. Sat. "This day there was a new moon and the weather changed for the better." And they were able to set off, but before doing so Johnson praised his hostess, saying, "She is the most accomplished lady I have found in the Highlands. She knows French, Musick and drawing, sews neatly, makes shellwork, and can milk cows; in short she can do everything. She talks sensibly....and can translate Erse poetry literally." Boswell found Mull to correspond "exactly with the idea which I had always had of it; a hilly country, diversified with heath and grass and many rivulets." But Johnson thought that it was "much worse than Skye....a most dolorous country" and he was "more out of humour today than he had been in the course of our tour." Boswell put this down to two causes, firstly the smallness of his horse (and Johnson was of a very large build) and secondly he had suffered a loss, though small in itself, but of consequence to him, while travelling the rugged steeps of Mull. "This was the loss of a large oak stick....brought from London. It was of great use....since his last illness in 1766 he has had weakness of his knees.... It had too the properties of a measuring; having two nails driven at one foot and one yard intervals. He had spoken only that morning of making a present of it to some museum; in return for the services it had done him....but he little thought he was so soon to lose it." As he was riding he had entrusted it "to a fellow to be delivered to our baggage man." Johnson was convinced it had been stolen. "It is not to be expected that any man in Mull who has got it will part with it. Consider, Sir, the value of such a piece of timber here!" After a long day they spent the night at the house of the McQuarries on Ulva. "We were agreeably surprised with the appearance of the master, whom we found to be intelligent, polite and much a man of the world." Johnson briefly mentions in his report that he discussed the ancient tradition of Mercheta Mulierum but Boswell gives more details saying that "McQuarrie insisted that Mercheta Mulierum....did really mean the privilege which a lord of the manor or a baron had, to have the first night of his vassal's wife." Johnson recalled that there was a "belief of such a custom having existed....in England....by which the eldest child does not inherit, from a doubt of his being the son of the tenant!"

Boswell gives other glimpses into their day-to-day life. "For fear of being overheard in the small Highland houses I often talked to him (Johnson) in such Latin as I could speak and with as much of an English accent as I could assume." And he explains an occurrence which "has been strangely misunderstood....it has erroneously been supposed that while on Ulva, his bed being too short for him, his feet, during the night, were in the mire; whereas he only said that, when he undressed, he felt his feet in the mire; that is, the clay floor of the room....was wet, in consequence of the windows being broken, which let in the rain."

Sun Oct 17th. They proceeded on their way to Inch Kenneth which lay on their route to the final destination of Iona. "Dr. Johnson's heart was cheered by the sight of a road marked with cartwheels, as on the Mainland; a thing he had not seen for a long time." Their host on Inch Kenneth, Sir Allan McLean, "had formed a commodious habitation....which had in his little appartments more things than I could enumerate in a page or two." This Boswell felt was due to his military background Dr. Johnson found books here. He said, "I do not like to read any thing on a Sunday, but that which is Theological; not that I would scrupulously refuse to look at anything which a friend should show me in a newspaper."

Johnson obviously felt at home with Sir Allan and showed so "much of the spirit of a Highlander, that he won Sir Allan's heart: indeed he had shewn it during the whole of our Tour....one night in Coll, he strutted about the room with a broadsword and target (shield), and made a formidable appearance; and another night I took the liberty to put a large blue bonnet on his head. His age, his size and his bushy grey wig with the covering on it presented the image of a venerable Senachi." However Johnson could not be prevailed upon to "partake of the social glass. One of his arguments against drinking appears to me not convincing." Johnson apparently believed it always altered a man's reason for the worse, whereas Boswell felt "that a man may be altered for the better; and his sprits may be exhilarated!" Boswell certainly enjoyed his glass of wine or sprits.

Mon. 18th Oct. They spent the day quietly with Sir Allan, preparing for their journey to Iona the following day. Young Col was about to leave to return to 'his lands' and Boswell reports on Johnson's praise of all that Col has done for them. "Col does everything for us; we will erect a statue to Col." "Yes," said I, "and we will have him as a pilot; we will have him as a fisherman, as a hunter, as a husbandman, as a physician." Later when Col told us "he could run down a greyhound....Johnson said, 'He is a noble animal. He is as complete an islander as the mind can figure....He is hospitable; and he has an intrepidity of talk, whether he understands the subject or not. I regret that he is not more intellectual.'"

Tues. 19th. Oct. "We parted from him (Col) with very strong feelings of kindness and gratitude; and we hoped to have had some future opportunity of proving to him the sincerity of what we felt; but in the following year he was unfortunately lost in the Sound between Ulva and Mull; and this imperfect memorial....is the only return which the uncertainty of human events has permitted us to make." The area of sea in which Col was lost is well known for the sudden changes in storm movement, and as we shall see later Lord Ullins daughter also died in this area.

As they left on their voyage to Iona they saw "the island of Staffa, at no very great distance, but could not land on it, the surge was so high on its rocky coast.... Sir Allan, anxious for the honour of Mull, was still talking of its wood.... Dr. Johnson said, 'Sir, I saw at Tobermorie what they called a wood, which I unluckily took for a heath. If you show me what I shall take for furze, it will be something.'"

As they approached Icolmkill the moon was out, the sea rough and as they passed between "black and gloomy rocks Dr. Johnson said, 'If this is not roving among the Hebrides, nothing is.'" The repetition of words which he had so often previously used made Boswell wonder how these present adventures would appear at a future date. "I have often experienced that scene through which a man has passed improve by lying in memory: they grow mellow....even harsh scenes acquire a softness by length of time." And he quotes Cowley in a footnote:

"Things which offend when present, and affright,
In memory, well painted, more delight."

On landing on Iona "the sacred place which as long as I can remember, I had thought on with veneration, Dr. Johnson and I cordially embraced.... Because of the lateness of the season, (we) were at times very doubtful whether we should be able to effect our purpose. To have seen it, even alone, would have given me great satisfaction; but the venerable scene was rendered much more pleasing by the company of my great and pious friend." And Boswell quotes Johnson's famous remark about "treading that illustrious Island" (see Dr. Johnson's account.)

They spent the first night "in some good hay strewn in a barn with a portmanteau for a pillow....when I awaked in the morning....I could not help smiling at the idea of the Chief of the McLeans, the great English Moralist, and myself, lying thus extended in such a situation."

Oct 20th Wed. "We were both disappointed, when we were shewn what are called the monuments of the Kings of Scotland, Ireland and Denmark, and of a King of France. There are only some gravestones flat on the earth, and we could see no inscriptions. How far short was this of the marble monuments, like those in Westminster Abbey, which I had imagined here!" Boswell noted Johnson's "peculiar accuracy of investigation detecting much traditional fiction, and many gross mistakes....he was provoked by people carelessly telling him, with the utmost readiness and confidence, what he found, in questioning them a little more, was erroneous."

Boswell had invested great personal expectations of Iona. "I had hoped that ever after having been in this Holy place, I should maintain an exemplary conduct. One has a strange propensity to fix upon some point of time from whence a better course of life may begin."

Later on that day, on landing on Mull once again they were "agreeably entertained" by Rev. Mr. Neil McLeod. "Johnson observed....he was the clearest headed man that he had met within the Western Islands." He seemed to be well acquainted with Dr. Johnson's writings and courteously said, "'I have been obliged to you, though I never had the pleasure of seeing you before.'"

Thur. 21st. Oct. Dr. Johnson continued to wage a friendly verbal battle with Sir Allan about Scotland. "Your country consists of two things, stone and water. There is indeed a little earth above the stone in places, but very little; and the stone is always appearing. It is like a man in rags; the naked skin is still peeping out." They proceeded on their way towards Lochbuy, stopping at mid-day to dine at the house of Dr Alexander McLean, "a physician....who was so much struck with the uncommon conversation of Dr Johnson that he observed to me, 'This man is just a hogshead of sense.'" After a very tedious ride "through....the most gloomy and desolate country," they arrived at Lochbuy.

"We had heard much of (the Laird of) Lochbuy's being a great roaring braggadocio, a kind of Sir John Falstaff....we found that they had swelled him up to a fictitious size." Col had described him as "quite a Don Quixote....he proved only to be a bluff, comely noisy old gentleman, proud of his hereditary consequence....and an hospitable landlord."

Fri. 22nd Oct. "Before Dr. Johnson came to breakfast, Lady Lochbuy (sister to Sir Allan) said, "He (Johnson) was a dungeon of wit....she proposed that he should have some sheep's head for breakfast. Sir Allan seemed displeased at his sister's vulgarity.... From a mischievous love of sport, I took the lady's part; and very gravely said, 'I think it is but fair to give him an offer of it'.... Sir Allan, finding the matter desperate, strutted about the room, and took snuff. When Dr. Johnson came in, she called to him, 'Do you choose any cold sheep's head, Sir?' 'No, Madam,' said he with a tone of anger and surprise." After a visit to the dungeons, where "Lochbuy had some years before taken upon him to imprison several persons. ....They bade adieu to Lochbuy and to our very kind conductor, Sir Allan McLean, on the shore of Mull."

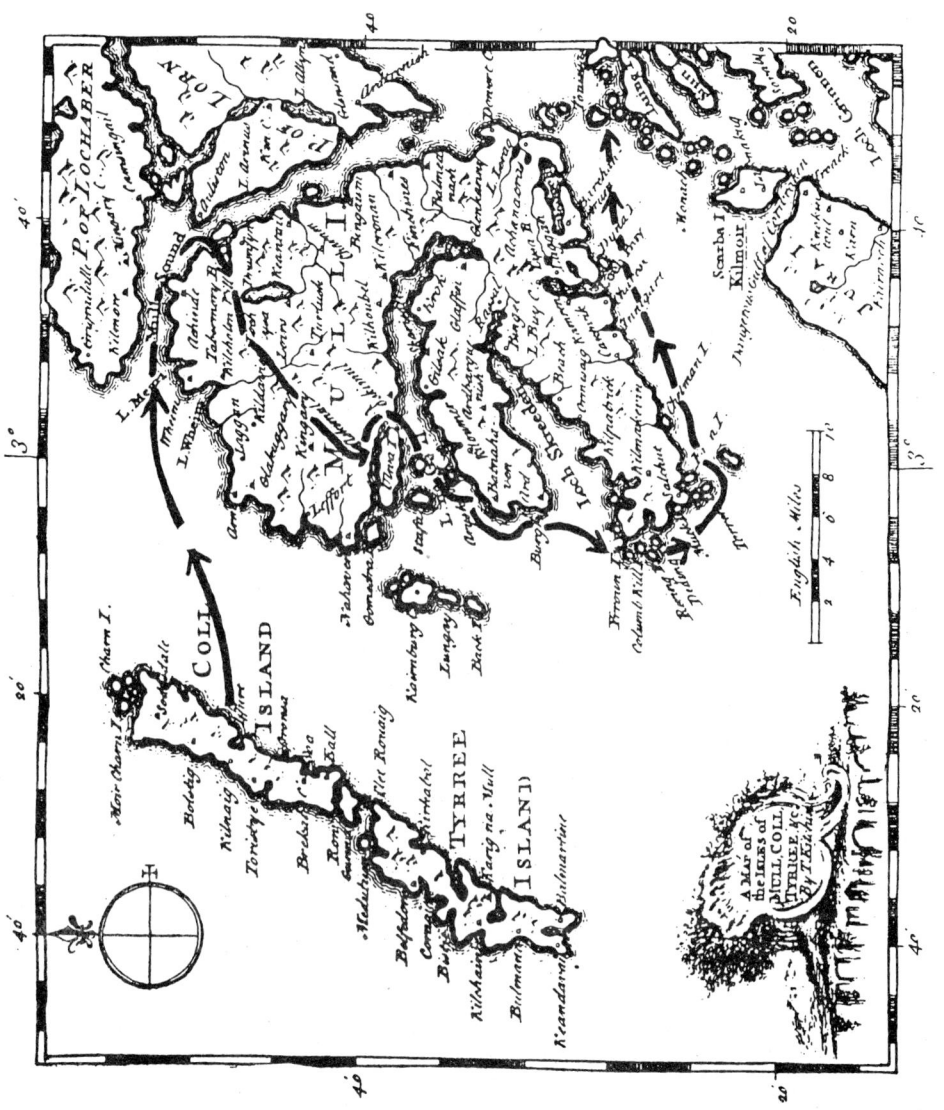

A map of Mull, Coll and Tyree, as well as Iona and the Treshnish Isles. Published by Thomas Kitchin at the begining of the 19th. century, with the route taken by Dr. Johnson and Boswell marked on it.

Faujas de St. Fond 1784.

Faujas de St. Fond was a French geologist, and really the first geologist to visit Staffa. In 1772 Sir Joseph Banks brought to St. Fond's notice the unusual formations on Staffa, which he had recently seen, and this aroused great interest in the Frenchman's mind so that he undertook the long and difficult journey across England and Scotland in order to see for himself the wonders of Staffa.

The following excerpts are from the translated account of his journey. Travelling through Dalmally on his way to Oban he noticed the Celtic design on the tombstones, describing them as "Sepulchral stones 15 inches broad and 3' 6" long, lying flat on the ground. These bas-reliefs are generally enclosed within a border, which is in itself a peculiar character, for it consists of Arabesques, loaded with interlaced ornaments, resembling filigree work, in which the strands cross each other in so many different directions that it is impossible to form a clear idea of what they meant to represent....some of the natives believe in the tradition that the stones mark the sepulchres of celebrated warriors, who lived in the times of the Old Kings of Scotland; others suppose that these tombs contain the remains of heroes of the North, at the epoch when the Danes made frequent incursions upon the coast of Scotland."

On arrival at Oban he described it as "a little hamlet by the sea consisting of six or seven scattered houses. The sea there abounds in fish and the herring industry, as well as that of salmon, form the principal resource of the place, for the natives only gather a little oats and hardly any barley, for the distillation of whisky. The salmon is dried in peat smoke, and then cut in pieces and put into barrels, which the Dutch come to buy in order to carry them to Spain and Italy as provision for Lent. They catch Oban salmon which weigh more than a hundred and fifty pounds; when the fish is well smoked and a little salted the people along the coast, as well as the fishermen, eat it raw as a dainty."

Having arrived on Mull, St. Fond's party set off for Torloisk where they planned to embark for Staffa, guided by two young Hebrideans who could "outrun our horses....their heads were decorated with a blue military bonnet, having a border of red, green and white, surmounted with one feather they wore with grace, a plaid having squares of different colours fastened on the shoulder and folded over the arm, with a waistcoat and jacket of the same stuff. Their thighs and legs were half-naked, but the latter were covered with a coloured buskin, while a convenient kind of shoe completed this Roman's dress."

Once again the hospitality at Torloisk was praised. "How attractive is this country; politeness, seasoned with the expressions and gestures of the most delicate feeling; we were here on the true soil of hospitality. All the inhabitants of the islands, though the population amounts to about six thousand souls, have only one family name, that of Maclean. They are distinguished by their Christian names, or by that of their residence....they are almost all shepherds or fishermen."

While staying at Torloisk with the Macleans, St. Fond gave details of the very substantial breakfast that he was offered at 10 o'clock in the morning:

"Slices of smoked beef
Cheese on trays of mahogany
Fresh eggs

Hash of salted herring
Butter, milk and cream
A sort of pap of oatmeal and water
Milk mixed with yolk of an egg, sugar and rum, drunk cold
Currant jelly, Conserve of myrtle (blaeberry jam)
Tea, coffee, Jamaica rum
Three sorts of bread."

A very elaborate style of meal, but probably a necessary type of breakfast when setting off for the hazards of a journey to Staffa or Iona. "They told me that my fellow travellers had sailed at 5 in the morning to visit Staffa....they had embarked with a friend of the (Maclean) family, and their own servants, in two small boats. But they had scarcely gone 5 leagues before the weather suddenly changed, and the sea became stormy. Mr. Maclean....was afraid they would not be able to land on the isle of Staffa....and had been obliged to take refuge in the isle of Iona.... On the third day from their departure....we went....to take a walk on the shore; at length, with the aid of a good glass, we descried them at a distance....they were so emaciated with fatigue, vexation and misery, were so in want of food and rest, and so uneasy, that they entreated us not to disturb them with questions until they were a little refreshed, and particularly relieved from a multitude of lice that tormented them most cruelly. 'Fly, fly from us,' said they, 'we have brought some good specimens of mineralogy, but our collection of insects is numerous and horrible.'"

"They recounted the circumstances of their unfortunate passage.... Having, at length, after many struggles and dangers, reached the isle of Staffa they found it still more difficult to effect a landing....the only two families living on this small island received them with the most effecting hospitality....and invited them to enter their hut, where they were ushered into the midst of six children, a woman, a cow, a pig, a dog and some fowls.... There was laid out for them a remnant of oaten straw, which had been used to litter the cow. This served as their seat, table and bed. A fire of hard peat, or rather ill-dried sod, lighted in the middle of the cabin, smoked them; at the same time it dried their clothes and served to cook, in an indifferent manner, some potatoes which, with a little milk, were the only article of food the place afforded, and these only in very small quantities. The provisions which they had brought with them were consumed at a single meal. On the second evening of their enforced stay on Staffa, a new incident occurred.... Detachments of lice approached from all sides to pay their respect to the new lodgers.... On the third day, their distress was at its height. They walked repeatedly round the island....to look for the approach of the boats, which at length made their appearance, and came to deliver our poor friends from their afflicting activity."

Mrs. Murray in her account adds further to our understanding of their plight, for her boatmen told her on her journey to Staffa that "two of the gentlemen had a violent quarrel and fought desperately on the stumps of the pillars near the mouth of Fingal's Cave. It was supposed the dispute originated in a difference of opinion, whether they should quit the island and venture on the yet stormy sea, or wait a further abatement of the tempest, at the risk of dying with hunger."

Despite these dangers and warnings from Maclean of Torloisk, and St. Fond's tendency to sea sickness, "he and Mr. Macdonald, an English Naval officer from Skye, and Mr. Thornton from the United States of America, set off for Staffa." "On a fine clear day, our seamen making Mr. Macdonald their interpreter....began to chant in chorus the songs of Ossian....they consisted of monotonous recitations ending in choruses equally monotonous....the oars, which kept time with the singing, tended to make the monotony more complete. I became drowsy and soon fell asleep."

On arriving on Staffa: "I ceased not to view, to review and to study this superb monument of nature, which in the regularity of its form bears so strong a resemblance to a work of art.... I took all the measurements of it, with the assistance of Mr. Macdonald.... During this time Mr Thornton took a drawing of the cave, which could been seen in a true point from the sea only.... This task was neither agreeable nor free from danger; for it required all the address of our seamen to keep for a few moments in front of the entrance, amidst the whirlpools and waves of a sea which seemed eager to engulf the frail skiff....it was necessary....to give rest at intervals to my dear Thornton, who was sick with the tossing.... After having noted down all the particulars respecting Fingal's Cave....I went to examine the other part of the island; and made a collection of different lavas, zeolites and other stones, which might serve to illustrate the natural history of the place.... Sir James Banks' draughtsman....has substituted, probably to give greater effect to the Cave, large masses of stone irregularly piled on each other on the right side of the kind of amphitheatre, which serves as a basis to that part of the grotto. But there is in reality nothing there except columns." (See accompanying print, which shows exactly what St. Fond describes.)

"Boo-shalla (a small islet off the main Part of Staffa) itself seems to be divided into two parts at high tides. It is composed of a number of eminences of prismatic basalt of a very regular kind, grouped together in bundles in some places, curved in others, and sometimes disposed in the manner of steps....this remarkable structure is not due to displacement, nor to the slipping down of large masses. It seems rather to be the effect of a more or less gradual cooling, and the material in shrinking appears to have undergone fantastic modifications and accidents comparable with those which may be observed in crystallization on a larger scale, though I am very far from considering the prismatic lava as the result of crystallization; on the contrary I regret that opinion....and the comparison I make here is only for the purpose of making it more intelligible, and has no relation but to the accidental varieties and different disposition of the forms."

A portrait of Faujas de St. Fond.

Another engraving from the late 18th century, depicting a most strange view of the interior of Fingal's Cave. In fact this looks as though the engraving has been printed the wrong way round. (This was something that happened when prints were 'pirated' by artists who had not actually been to the site and seen the subject for themselves.) Or it may have been as St. Fond himself suggested that 'Sir James Banks, draughtsman... has substituted, probably for greater effect to the cave, large masses of stone irregularly piled on each other.... but there is in reality, nothing there except columns.'

John Knox. 1786

A Tour Through the Highlands of Scotland and the Hebride Isles including St. Kilda.

John Knox was a Scottish philanthropist and, after retiring from his work as a bookseller in London, he devoted himself to the improvement of Fisheries and Manufactories of Scotland. Between 1764-1775, he made 10 tours of Scotland. The Highland Society of London gave him support and encouragement. He was a leading member of the British Society formed in Scotland in 1786 and he published Observations on the Northern Fisheries with a Discourse on the Expediency of Establishing Fishing Stations or Small Towns in the Highlands of Scotland and Hebride Isles. The British Fishery Society collected £7000 for the purpose of establishing fishing villages and commissioned John Knox to make " a more extensive journey in the Highlands and Isles than had ever been performed by an individual." It was proposed that on the 400 miles of coast from the Mull of Cantire (Kentyre) to Dornoch Firth, and 600 miles of the Hebride "to erect 40 stations or fishing towns, at 25 miles of each other, more or less as circumstances suit, to consist of 16 houses of 2 storeys and 2 rooms, with an inn, and a school house and an acre or half an acre to each, each town to cost £2000."

Leaving Oban on June 29th 1786 he travelled on foot and boat, completing the journey to Cape Wrath in 6 months. He describes Mull as being "24 Scots or 36 English miles in length, and nearly the same in breadth, and having 7000 inhabitants....£10 per annum is allowed for the free schools, but being generally run by old domestic servants (they) are not sufficiently qualified for the charge committed to them.... Mull sends out 1500 black cattle at £3 a head....200 deer range among the hills, but no horses....there is no appearance of a regular well built village, nor of manufactures of even spinning to any extent....one half of the women are perfectly idle, except in the harvest time." Knox advocates "one market town situated on the Sound of Mull, and another on the West side of the Island, which would be attended with the most beneficial consequences to the proprietors." He suggests that Tobermory is "capacious for a number of large ships."

He crossed the North West side of the island and embarked with John Campbell of Knock (see Mrs. Murray), who owned land around Tobermory, in order to investigate the West side of Mull and Staffa as well as the Ross of Mull. Travelling through the Loch Tuath he passed the Treshnish Isles and Inch Kenneth on the way to Loch Levin (Loch Scridain). They encountered a great storm between 26th. and 30th. July, the worst in living memory which shook "the corn from the roots and broke the tops of the potatoes." Knox felt that Lochbuy could be made to be a good harbour, and he was "invited into a cottage and presented with a snuff-mull and heard great news....that the Duke of Argyle was going to make a canal at Loch Crinan and build many towns in the Highlands." He also suggested that Packet Boats "should be established between the Hebrides and the mainland.... The smuggling vessels which have been seized by the Revenue cutters would serve admirably for this purpose."

John Knox also made some interesting comments on Dr. Johnson: "He was no antiquarian; and seems to have had very little taste for botany and the various branches of natural history. Combining these disadvantages, the Doctor it may be supposed was ill-qualified for explorating....but these defects were only secondary considerations, when compared to his disposition and temper respecting that country and people. He set out under incurable impressions of a natural prejudice and religious prejudice and literary jealousy ....From a writer of such abilities, and such prejudices, the natives of Scotland had reason to expect a shower of arrows without mercy....they were ready to fall upon him as one man the moment that his book appeared, their minds charged with sentiments of indignity, resentment and revenge.... He sustained the shock with firmness and when threatened with corporal chastisement by an eminent historian, he threw down the gauntlet, and provided himself with a cudgel 6ft. long, and a club at the end of it.... If, however, we make allowances for the Doctor's bodily and mental infirmities, by which I mean his dogmatical disposition and strong prejudices, the observations and conclusions upon what he said may be considered as valuable acquisition to the History of North Britain. I have read his book again and again, travelled with him from Berwick to Glenelg....sailed with him from Glenelg to Raasay, Sky, Rum, Coll, Mull and Icolmkill; but have not been able to correct him in any matter of consequence....admired his accuracy, the precision and the justness of what he advances, respecting both the country and the people....were the book stripped of some illiberal epithets and of his lame conjectures respecting Gaelic genius, it would make an excellent supplement to the invaluable writings of the traveller (Mr. Pennant) who proceeded him."

A 19th century view of the entrance to the harbour at Oban, showing the nothern end of the isle of Kererra. The land and seascape would have appeared the same to John Knox in 1786, but there would have been no steamships.

Thomas Campbell 1795.

Thomas Campbell, the poet, set off from Glasgow on May 18th. 1795, to work as a tutor for a Highland family, who were connections of his. Writing to his friend, Hamilton Paul, he said:

"Mull is to be my place of residence this summer. I go to stay with a young widow lady, a namesake and connection of my own.... I expect in Mull a calm retreat for study and the muse. From Oban I crossed over to Mull and in the course of a long summer day, traversed the whole length of the island which must be 30 miles, with not a footpath to direct me. At times I lost all trace of my way and had no guide but the sun going westward. About twilight, however, I reached The Point of Cailleach, the house of my hostess, Mrs. Campbell of Sunipol* a worthy sensible widow, who treated me with great kindness. At first I felt melancholy in this situation and wrote a poem on my exile, called <u>The Elergy</u>

"The Tempest blackens on the dusky moor
And billows lash the long resounding shore.
In pensive mood I roam the desert ground,
And vainly sigh for scenes no longer gound.
O whither fled....
The classic haunts of youth forever gay?

*The house of Sunipol is clearly visible to anyone sailing from Tobermory to Staffa or Coll or Tiree; it stands near the shore in the centre of the bay immediately before you turn that point of Mull where you first get a view of Staffa.

Far different scenes allure my wondering eye -
The white wave foaming to the distant sky;
The cloudy heavens unblest by summer's sky,
The sounding storm that sweeps the rugged isle,
The chill bleak summit of eternal snow.
The wide wild glen - the pathless plains below;
The dark blue rocks, in barren grandeur piled;
The cuckoo, sighing to the pensive wild."

July 1795

Hamilton Paul said, "When Campbell first went to the island of Mull, he was affected by *ennui* and the *maladie du pays*." By June 14th he wrote again to Hamilton: "Perhaps my date is wrong, I forget the day of the month, owing to absence of books and paper. There is no paper on Mull. I thus grow weary of life and Mull, God knows, is a place ill-suited to rub off the rust of a dull temper. Every scene you meet is to be marked by sublimity and the wild majesty of nature, but it is only fit for the haunts of the damned in bad weather. I continued from May 21st till a few days (ago), when a most delicious alteration in weather somewhat roused my spirits."

On the 18th he wrote again to Hamilton: "We savages in Mull never keep any reckon of the months. I believe it to be the 18th!" Later on he had the chance to visit Staffa and Iona which "filled me with emotions of pleasure.... When I looked into the Cave of Staffa, I regretted nothing." The summit of the island is a rich plain "of grass and corn in the centre of which stands a lonely hut, in appearance very like the abode of a hermit or savage; the pillars are not a random curiosity broken and irregular, they are exactly similar and well proportioned as if the hand of an artist had carved them out of the walls with a chisel....there is a wildness and sublimity in them beyond what art can produce.... We entered the mouth of the cave with a peal of bagpipes, which made a most tremendous echo."

Will Beattie M.D., who edited Thomas Campbell's <u>Life and Letters</u>, feels that his stay in Mull was ideal "for laying in a stock of poetic imagery, and he fully availed himself of the opportunity....he had a heath-clad wilderness - bleak, lifeless - and broken into numberless glens, strewn with rocks and scantily clothed with copsewood; from the dusky covert of which he could observe the wild deer darting forth at intervals.... Blue rocks fringed with wild flowers, rising in huge, often grotesque masses through the purple heath; streams and torrents winding peacefully through deep grassy glens or dashing in clouds of spray over some rugged precipice; the shrill pipe of the curlew - the blythe carol of the lark overhead - the screams of the eagle from his eyrie in the rocks - the bleating of goats from the steep pastoral acclivities - the crowing of the heath-cock - the barking of the sheep dog, the casual step or shot of the deer stalker."

Using an incident which Campbell heard from a family he knew on Mull, who owned a parrot, he wrote a poem about a parrot from the Spanish Main:

"A parrot from the Spanish Main,
Full young and early eyed, came o'er
With bright wings to the bleak domain
Of Mulla's shore.

To spicey groves where he had won
His plumage of resplendent hue;
His native fruits, and sky, and sun,
He bade adieu....

At last when blue and seeming dumb
He scolded, laughed and spoke no more,
A Spanish stranger chanced to come
To Mulla's shore.

He hailed the bird in Spanish speech;
In Spanish speech the bird replied,
Flapped round his cage with joyous screech,
Dropt down, and died."

    He tells too of an amusing incident which occurred on one of his 'Botanizing' excursions. He climbed over the iron railings around a burial ground in order to read the epitaphs. He was seen by some crofters, and a few days later he became aware of them looking at him in "mournful seriousness." At last the grandmother explained that he "could not live long for his wraith had been seen." He asked where it had appeared and they were much relieved to hear, "It was not my wraith, but myself you saw."

    The poem for which he is best known is that of <u>Lord Ullin's Daughter</u>, which tells the story of a young couple eloping across Loch Na Gael (Loch Na Keal) from Ulva, which is presumed to be based on factual evidence:

"Now who be he would cross Lochgyle*
This dark and stormy water?
O, I'm the chief of Ulva's Isle
And this Lord Ullin's daughter."

*Loch na Keal.

The storms that can sweep down from Ben More and in from the Atlantic can be very severe and very sudden. So the story of the tragedy which overcame them is very possible, particularly remembering Johnson and Boswell's friend Col who was drowned in much the same area.

Another of his well-known poems, Glenara, concerned the story of one of the Macleans of Duart, who placed his wife, a sister of the Duke of Argyle, on a rock in the Sound of Mull, because she talked too much. This rock, which is dry and above water at low tide, is completely covered at high tide. Her husband ordered a mock funeral to be performed in order to conceal the murder. However she was rescued by one of her brothers and taken to Inverary. Her husband escaped punishment until he was 89 years of age, and then retribution finally caught up with him, for another brother, Sir John Campbell, was able at long last to get his revenge and slay his cruel brother-in-law in Edinburgh. The rock is still called Lady Rock and is still visible at low tide in the Sound of Mull.

Campbell does seem to have laid up a stock of 'Poetic Imagery' as Will Beatie suggested, for he used another famous natural local feature in his poem, Gertrude of Wyoming, when he refers to the Whirlpool at Corrievrechan. Commenting on the actual whirlpool, Campbell said, "I have often listened with great delight to the sound of this vortex at the distance of many leagues. When the weather is calm and the adjacent sea scarcely heard on these picturesque shores, its sound, which is like the sound of innumerable chariots, creates a magnificient and fine effect." The lines of the poem alluding to the whirlpool are as follows:

"But who is he that yet a dearer land
Remembers over hills and far away?
Green Albyn. 'What though he no more survey
The ships at anchor on the quiet shore,
Thy pellochs* rolling from the mountain bay,
Thy lone spulchral cairn upon the moor,
And distant isles that hear the loud Corbrechan roar.'"

*pellochs - Gaelic name for porpoise

Visitors in the interior of Fingal's Cave, having arrived on a calm day by a small sailing boat, can easily examine the cave without the danger of getting very wet. An early C18th print, which, it is interesting to note, occurs in two forms, one, as in this case, with the visitors in Highland dress, and the other with the figures in 'English' dress. (Was there, even as early as 1800, a distinct difference in the tourist trade?)

Dr. T. Garnett M.D. 1798.

Dr. Garnett was a member of the Royal Medical, Physical and Natural History Society of Edinburgh, and in 1798 he wrote a book entitled <u>Observations on a Tour through the Highlands and Part of the Western isles of Scotland</u>.

From Dr. Garnett we learn a great deal about the hardships which the people of Mull were experiencing at the end of the 18th century. Dr. Garnett arrived from Oban, via the ferry to the Isle of Kerrera, which they crossed on a "very indifferent road" and then took another ferry boat across to Mull, arriving near Achnacraig. The news that a Doctor had come to Mull soon spread and, while visiting the Rev. Alexander Frazer, the Minister of the parish of Torosay, he tended to "a dozen patients from the small village of Killean." Typhus fever was rife at the time.

Garnett pointed out how difficult it was for the inhabitants of Mull to obtain salt, an essential part of the herring fishing which could have been such a great financial gain to them at the time. "Great numbers of them (herring) were caught last year and would have been sold to great advantage but the greater part were suffered to rot, for want of this article (i.e. salt). The duty on salt is so high that the herring cannot be cured unless it (the duty) is taken off. This having been represented to the Government, the salt is now sold free of duty, for the purpose of curing fish only; but this privilege requires so many forms that it is impossible to comply with them."

Those who needed salt had to go to Oban and make an oath at the custom house that the salt would only be used for curing. They also had to give a bond, which was not discharged until they returned with the herrings and the remaining salt that was left over. As Oban is at least twenty miles away, and much farther for those on the West coast of Mull, "the people will never go to the custom house for salt till the herring appear in the lochs; from the well-grounded fear that the fishing may fail." When they did appear the weather might be bad and the salt damaged in transit and valuable time lost before they could return to their fishing. The result of this bureaucracy was, of course, to resort to smuggled salt for which "they pay high" but at least they save the "tedious formalities and loss of time."

Garnett also shows, by means of a sketch and verbal description, exactly how grain was ground into flour by means of a quern. "The quern consists of two circular pieces of stone, generally of grit or granite, about twenty inches in diameter. In the lower stone is a wooden peg, rounded at the top; on this the upper stone is nicely balanced, so as just to touch the lower one by means of a piece of wood fixed in a large hole in this upper piece, but which does not fill the hole, room for feeding the mill being left on each side: it is so nicely balanced that though there is some friction from the contact of the two stones, yet a very small momentum will make it revolve several times, when it has no corn in it. The corn being dried, two women get down on the ground, having the quern between them; the one feeds it while the other turns it round, relieving each other occasionally, and singing Celtic songs all the time."

A Quern

Garnett described the cottages on Mull as being "much worse than any we had seen on the mainland. They usually consist of two wretched appartments, one of which serves the family for parlour kitchen and hall....the other harbours the animals. The floor is bare earth, with a fire of peat in the centre over which hangs an iron pot. In many parts of Mull, particularly near Aros, they use a wicker door, or osier hurdle." Sometimes the small opening which serves as a window had a "thick pane of glass" or a wooden shutter. The cottages "are generally thatched with fern or heath....kept on by ropes of heath stretched by stones tied on the ends."

He commented on the lack of enclosures for crops, oats, barley and flax, which necessitated a herdsmen to prevent the cattle eating the crops. He felt it was a pity that they were not taught some useful employment which they could practise while they tended the cattle. They could knit stockings or set the teeth of cards (for spinning). Ironically, he reports favourably on the first signs that sheep are spreading: "The tops of even the highest hills used formerly to be covered with black cattle, very few sheep being kept, but now the hills are stocked with sheep and the low marshy grounds with black cattle." This improvement, as Garnett saw it, was soon to prove anything but an improvement to the people of Mull, for as more and more sheep made their appearance they required more and more land, so that the crofters were driven off their traditional grazing lands, and eventually from their homes by heartless and often absent landlords. However, Garnett could not be expected to be able to see the long term results of these first sheep, and he was very concerned about the social conditions which forced the crofter, once the winter was over, to catch white fish, which he then transported in an open boat 200 miles to Glasgow (this was before the opening of the Crinan Canal). "He sold his catch for £12-£15 and bought meal and more tackle and rowed back to Mull. ....The autumn calls his attention again to the field, the usual round of disappointment, fatigue and distress awaits him: he then drags through a wretched existence.... In times of war he was even worse off, being indiscriminately pressed (into the Army), without regard to cases of circumstances" so that the families they left behind, unable to pay the rent, were turned out of their homes.

The kelp industry (the burning of seaweed in order to produce alkali for the manufacture of glass and soap) was at its height at this time, and proved very profitable for the islanders for a time during the Wars with France; but once the normal imports were re-established the demand for kelp from Mull came to an end. While Garnett was on Mull he "believed not less than 500 tons (of kelp) are annually made in Mull," the cost of manufacture being approximately 30/- a ton. Kelpers earned 7½p a week, which was a fair wage. The Seven Years' War with France and The American War of Independence caused a decrease in imported barilla (the previous source of alkali) and the price rose to £22 a ton. (During the Napoleonic war, the price was £10 a ton until 1822.) So for sixty-six years the Hebrides enjoyed a very marketable industry. But the islanders suffered a great deal when this source of income was no longer available because they had become used to a better standard of living, and the birthrate had also increased.

On July 17th Garnett and his party proceeded to Aros; that road being "chiefly made by the Government is very good, indeed it is almost the only passable road in the island." They passed castle Dowart (Duart) "....now in ruins....which affords accommodation to a small party of soldiers sent in from Fort William to prevent smuggling." About thirteen miles from Achnacraig they passed "the ruins of an old church, near which were several tombstones, some of them very ancient but several modern." This must have been the Chapel at Pennygowan.

They were "hospitably entertained" by Mr Maxwell, factor to the Duke of Argyle, who sent a guide with them to Torloisk. (Sacheverell had also been entertained at Aros 110 years earlier). Garnett mentioned in passing that Tobermory is a "village lately built by The British Society for encouraging fisheries who have a property of 2000 acres....Tobermory....possesses a fine bay....is situated in the track of shipping...." The Society began to form this village in the year 1788, and a custom-house and post office were established here in the year 1791. The village consists of about twenty houses, built with stone and lime and covered with slate (see Daniell's aquatint of Tobermory 1813, front cover).

The path from Aros to Torloisk "is the most rugged, stoney and mountainous I ever saw." But on arrival at Torloisk the hospitality is once again enthusiastically spoken of. "Mr. Maclean, whose house is large and elegant and unquestionably the best in the island....procured us a boat belonging to some of his tenants in the island of Gometra" in order to visit Staffa, but on July 18th, "the morning being very stormy, we could not venture to visit Staffa....but were entertained with the most friendly hospitality....and gave me an opportunity of extending my notes." These mention the change in the geology of the rocks from those at Aros to those at Torloisk, and comments on the seams of coal at Beinanini, the Ross of Mull, Brolass and Gribun.

Another of Garnett's interests was in proverbs and folklore, and he recounts the origin of the local proverb: "What a fool I was to burn my harp for her (him)," which indicates ingratitude from someone who has benefited from your generosity. In former times a celebrated harpist was married to an exquisite beauty; next to his wife, the harp was his pride and joy. On a visit to a sick relation, she fainted because of the cold and storm. In order to warm her he kindled a fire and burnt his harp to feed the flames. A young gentleman passing was distressed to see her condition and offered food and spirits. She revived and joined in 'animated' conversation with the gentleman, whom, it transpired, she had known in her early life, while being brought up by her grandmother on a nearby island. On her grandmother's death she had left the island and returned to Mull, and they had never met since. Now, however, their romance was reawakened, and by means of a ruse, they gave the husband the slip and eloped together. Hence his exclamation, "Fool that I was to burn my harp for thee."

July 19th was still stormy, and Dr. Garnett's words sound almost like an echo of Dr. Johnson's while he was staying at Inch Kenneth with Sir Allan and his ladies. "The Society at Torloisk and the ladies (meant) we were not disposed to complain. It was not without surprise, I must confess, that on an Island in the Hebrides far from the gay and busy world, we met with elegant society, and every comfort and convenience that could have been procured in the capital with far more sincerity and hospitality. Mr. Maclean's family consisted, besides himself, of his lady, Mrs Maclean's sister and a female friend of theirs, both highly accomplished and agreeable."

On July 20th they finally set off for Staffa. "On going on board we witnessed another proof of Mrs Maclean's goodness, for we found wine for ourselves and spirits for the boatmen and a plentiful supply of provisions for us all." They were rowed out between Ulva and Gometera, where a boat can only pass at high water, then a light breeze sprang up and they were able to hoist a sail. "At a distance of three miles from Staffa, we heard what we supposed to be the report of guns which repeated at regular intervals, perhaps every half minute." They imagined a ship in distress, but they were soon to find on rounding the farther side of Staffa that the sound was made by water being forced into a cavity with great force, so that "it condensed the air in the cavity....when the force of the wave was exhausted and its immense pressure removed the spume of condensed air forced out the water in the form of a fine white froth, like smoke, accompanied with a report similar to firing a cannon." It is interesting that Garnett is the only one of the travellers, with the exception of Sir Walter Scott and Mrs. Murray, who refers to this extraordinary phenomenon, which at one time is said to have contained a round stone weighing about 5lbs. It is known as *Gunna-Mor* (Big Gun).

Garnett described the pillars at the top of the island as being of a "dark purple hue inclined to black, but in many places richly coloured with green, yellow or orange....produced by different species of lichen." His description of Fingal's Cave, "where regularity is the only part in which Art pretends to excel Nature, but here Nature has shown that when she pleases she can set man at nought even in this respect," is similar to other comments made at the turn of the 18th century.

They continued on their journey to Iona. Garnett mentioned that, of the altar, referred to by Sacheverell, "there are now no remains." He recalled that Pennant, when he visited in 1769, had only "a very small portion left." Later he gave a very detailed description of the gravestones and mentioned the famous Beaton's of Pennygael in Mull who "were physicians....one of them was sent for to attend one of the Kings of Scotland." His motto being "be cheerful, temperate and early risers," Garnett felt "that the whole College of Physicians could not have devised a better rule."

Referring to the valuable books once housed in the library on Iona and mentioned by Pennant, "It is said that some of the manuscripts were carried to Inverary and that one of the Dukes of Montague found some of them in the shops of that time being used for snuff paper." What an end to such historic records!

Gylen Castle on the southern end of the isle of Kererra, near where Dr. Garnett would have embarked for the second time, on his way to Mull, after having travelled on the 'very indifferent road' across the island of Kererra.

Dr. John Leyden. 1800

Dr. John Leyden, physician and poet, was also editor of the Scots Magazine in 1802; but it is chiefly as a geologist that he is important in his connection with Mull. His Journal of a Tour in the Highlands and Western Islands of Scotland in 1800, consists of "a collection of a great deal of valuable information regarding literary antiquities and traditions of the Highlands. Many curious observations also appear on the Ossian Controversy, which still exercised the literati of the time," says James Swinton in the prefatory note to the Journal, which also mentions Leyden's works Scottish Descriptive Poems and Scenes of Infancy, Descriptive of Teviotdale.

Sir Walter Scott, Leyden's friend and biographer, also commented on the Journal. "In this tour he visited all the remarkable places of that interesting part of his native country and, diverging from the common route, visited what are called the rough bounds of the Highlands, and investigated the decaying traditions of Celtic Manners and Stories, which are yet preserved in the wild districts of Móidart and Knoidart.... It is remarkable that, after a long and painful research in quest of original passages of the poems of Ossian, he adopted an opinion more favourable to their authenticity than has lately prevailed in the literary world." (See Jules Verne, The Green Ray.)

July 21st 1800: With two German friends, Vincke and Burgsdorff, Leyden crossed from Oban to Auchna-craig on a night that was "raw and misty so that we could hardly distinguish the shore of Morven." The next day, July 22nd, Leyden commented on the geology of Mull. At Auchna-craig he noticed that the "threshold and some parts of the house were floored with blue limestone dotted like pyrites, as if it had been stuck full of nails." And he also said that "the huts of the peasants in Mull are deplorable. Some of the doors are hardly four feet high, and the houses of sods are scarcely twelve feet long." The lack of any outlet for smoke made the women "more squalid and dirty than the men." After procuring a guide at Aros, they "proceeded by the side of Loch-na Gaul (Loch-na-Keal) for Ulva. "In our passage by the side of the lake we saw a natural wall of basalt, of the thickness of two feet or more, both surfaces of which nearly resembled a natural wall in regularity." What today geologists would call a dyke.

July 23rd. Due to misty weather Leyden did not accompany his German friends to Staffa; they, "however, set out with true German intrepidity, carrying a piper along with them, whose notes we heard long after they had ceased to be seen, and fortunately stumbled upon the island of Staffa and with greater good fortune stumbled upon the way back, though not without tedious deviation."

However, on July 24th, a much more promising day, he set off for Staffa, picking up a bagpiper from Ulva "and soon beheld the white clouds of vapour rolling away in confusion and the lofty top of Ben More, emerging amid broken and shattered columns, which seemed to tumble down his bare sides, glittering with micaceous schistus like silver.

"We landed on Staffa at the Long Cave, through which we proceeded a considerable way, till the passage became very dark and extremely narrow.... The columns near the top are bent precisely like the ribs of a vessel.... The colours of the columns are gray, black, and dark brown. Some of them are black and scorched, almost approaching the nature of volcanic scoriae. On the east side (of the island) the columns are not so regular as on the south and west, but they contain numerous zeolites of different colours, chiefly green and white, sometimes crystallised and sometimes soft and striated like schoil, chalcedony, garnets and martial jasper. We took some zeolites off the rocks, which nearly resembled a petrified cockle.... On the little rock or rather island of Boo-shalla, the columns are extremely perfect, and their trunkated ends rise up regularly above each other to the top like the steps of a stair.

Booshala, or as it is known today, The Herdsman, a 19th century engraving from *The Lady's Magazine*, showing the small isle which lies just off the Causeway, leading to Fingal's Cave.

"The Cave of Fingal, termed in Gaelic *An-na-vine,* or the melodius cave, is grand almost beyond imagination." Like Garnett, he found the colours varied from "reddish dark" to "black....the solid part of the wall over the entrance, is covered with moss beautifully variegated, but chiefly yellow." Having collected specimens and "viewed the island on every side, we seated ourselves on a rock, and the piper, playing a martial pibroch, we soon saw ourselves surrounded with sheep, cows and among the rest of the animals we saw three deer which had been placed on the island, and which seemed perfectly tame." A very different observation from that of Mrs. Murray a few years later.

Leyden was told by one of "our rowers" that "in a storm the waves rise almost to the top of the basalt columns and cover the whole island with foam." He also reported that "There is a tradition that formerly the island was three times as large but, being founded on columns, was undermined and sank in the waves. The sloping base of the columns on the West side and the length of the caves, especially Boat Cave, seem to have given origin to the idea."

"In a dead calm of the most sickening heat we rowed away for Iona....as we approached we saw a number of swains and nymphs on the shore; neither beautiful nor elegant, instead of tending their flocks and herds, very busy making kelp." He found the "small irregular huts....much superior to the huts on Mull....being composed of rough granite and porphyry." In his description of the Abbey he mentions that the windows are "pretty entire" and that "the steeple tower is almost perfect, and displays a very elegant Gothic window, the interior part of which consists of a number of circular figures, flourished diagonally."

Leyden mentions two other interesting features; having visited St. Oran's Chapel and the Nunnery they "saw the stones which are to hasten the end of the world....when the lower hollowed stone is worn out by turning them round, the end of the world is to ensue." Pennant also mentioned these stones, saying they were turned "according to the course of the sun." There seems to be no current record of their existence, so either they have been mislaid or the prophecy was untrue. The second feature mentioned is that of "a kind of font (at the door of the Abbey) sunk in the ground, concerning which there is a tradition that whenever it is emptied of rain water which it generally contains, a northern breeze immediately springs up."

Leyden climbed Dun-I and reported that "the two extremities of the island rise in clusters of white rocks, which consist chiefly of trapp, gray schistis, and schorlaceous schistis."

To return to the mainland he procured a boat which was "only a clumsy open coble rowed by four unskilled fishermen....there was no room to lie....we coasted along the low shore of the Ross, the rocks of which consist almost entirely of red and gray granite and porphyry." Having sailed through the Sound of Fechan and proceeded along the East shore of Mull, they found their boat "had not been sufficiently victualled....we hove to near Carsaig Bay, and landed among a strange cluster of rocks, where we found a hut and procured some goats' milk and goats' cheese, but no bread."

During the night the fishermen amused us with singing....they likewise related the story of MacPhael of Colonsay, with whom the Mermaid of the Gulf of Corrievrekin fell in love; snatching him down to her palace in Davie's locker....she bore him several children....but carrying him one day near the land, he sprang suddenly ashore and deserted his she-goddess. This last story however, seemed to amuse us much more than the fishermen, for they appeared to be dreadfully afraid of some sea-spirits' appearance from some stormy recesses of the dark shore of Mull. I know not how far they might be to the taste of the sea nymph, but I apprehended there was little danger of their being ravished by a land one." This fear of sea spirits occurs again in R.L. Stevenson's short story, Merry Men.

A romantic view of Dunstaffnage Castle, at that time inhabited (see the smoking chimney), with a group of villagers and goats dancing in the foreground (c.1800) and looking very much as it would have done when Dr. J. Leyden passed it on route to Oban.

Mrs. Murray. 1800.

Mrs Murray, the author of a <u>Companion and Useful Guide</u>, was a most adventurous traveller, and was the first woman to travel on her own without travelling companions in the Western Isles. Her comments on her adventures while on Mull, Iona, Staffa and Ulva, show her very wide and varied interests - in farming, the local people, the geology, plant life, and a general fascination with the local way of life. Her comments are also free of much of the moralizing tone which can be detected in many of the early travellers. A woman travelling on her own was obviously an unusual sight for the inhabitants, and her descriptions of their wary approach towards her are so very different from the experiences of William Wordsworth and J. Wilson thirty or forty years later. Presumably tourism had increased so much by the 1830s that the islanders had realized the financial benefit which was being brought to their shores by the great increase in steamer travel.

On July 23rd 1800, Mrs. Murray set sail for Aros on Mull from Oban in the Excise cutter. "The entrance to the Sound of Mull is beautiful, Morven on the one hand, the Isle of Mull on the other; Duart Castle forming a fine object on the shore of the latter and the old Castle of Ardtonish, with the bold cliffs, on the former. Mists floating on the sides of Majestic mountains in a style I had never seen before, it was like Ossian's 'shadowy breeze that poured its dark wave over the grass'". As there was no breeze to continue the journey, she spent the night at Ardtonish, and visited the ruined castle and told of the finding of an enormous key, "at least a yard long, the breadth of the wards were more than a foot....so heavy that one man could but carry it. This surely must have been the master key of the castle." Unfortunately by mistake the local smith melted it down, "he thought it a great pity such fine iron should remain useless, and he therefore had made tools of it."

Later Mrs. Murray was rowed across the Sound of Mull to Aros in a small boat, accompanied by Gaelic songs from the rowers, and was entertained by Mr and Mrs Maxwell, who were holding a gala dinner. The Maxwells advised her to set off for Staffa before the weather changed, so with two Highlanders to accompany her she started, "dressed in a red leather cap trimmed with brown fur, and a habit of tartan, such as is worn by the 42nd Regiment of Highlanders, mounted on a white horse "with a Fingalian stick in her hand....thus moved Mrs. Murray's first cavalry expedition in the Isle of Mull, laughable as it was. She passed the house at Knock where a gentleman called Campbell lived "who, at eighty, had shot a deer near the summit of Ben More" (this gentleman is also mentioned by John Knox, earlier on in this collection.)

Riding along the margin of Loch na Keal she found "the road exceedingly rough but....I found growing....fine barley and oats, as any I ever saw in South Britain; the brushwood adds beauty to this terrific pass." On arriving at a small village, the women were extremely curious at the arrival of a woman traveller and "brought me a basin of fine milk." She travelled to Torloisk, where Mrs. M'lean advised her to take advantage of the very favourable day and provided her with food and drink and a small boat with four rowers. Mrs Murray squeezed in and they had a smooth journey to Staffa. "I was in ecstasy at the very regular pillars and the elevated dome over the great caves." She thought the form of the Boat Cave "some-what resembling a barn door.... What gives a very singular beauty to the South part of Staffa is that....not a fallen or loose piece of rock or rubbish of any kind is seen....I remained in silent amazement...." She said on entering Fingal's Cave, "When I got within it I forgot the world and everything it contains....Staffa produced the highest pitch of solemn, pious, enthusiastic sensation I ever felt or ever can feel, in this my house of clay." From the inside of Fingal's Cave she admired "the prospect of Iona's Cathedral in perspective, through the arch of the Cave, at a great distance across the sea."

She also mentions the fact that some visitors have suggested that the weight of Staffa's head is too heavy for its legs, having bent them on the east side of Fingal's Cave. She dined on the horizontal pillars of Clamshell Cave - "never again shall I have such a dining room." Having dined she climbed up to the plateau above and, feeling giddy, "I laid myself flat on my breast, and thus crept forward till I got my head over the edge of the roof rising from the arch of the cave."

There were three red deer, including a stag, on the island which was at the time owned by Ranald McDonald of Boisdale, and she imagined that "had the wild stag taken a fancy to have lifted me on his horns, when lying flat on the ground, with my head over Fingal's Cave, and tipped me over, what an uncommon death I would have had!" Many stories are told of the terrors endured by solitary herdsman (on the isle of Staffa) but two years later in 1802, she met a man who had lived on Staffa and said there "was no truth in the assertions of his pot shaking on the fire, from any effects of the sea on the island." "In the year 1800 I was the ninth female stranger who had ventured to Staffa, but none of them had gone valiantly alone as I did."

She also told the story of Faujas de Saint Fond, the geologist and naturalist, who, with a gentleman from London, Count

A...from Italy and a Mr. M from Ireland were "detained on Staffa for four days by bad weather, with only one day's provisions....two of the gentlemen....had a violent quarrel, and fought desperately on the stumps of the pillars near the mouth of Fingal's Cave," probably over the question of whether they should "venture on the yet stormy sea or risk dying with hunger." From Mrs. Murray we also learn of the Irishmen who removed the stone from Thunder Cave; this stone caused a sound like a cannon shot when the force of the sea expelled the air in the hole, which echoed round the island. (See also Garnett's account.)

Apparently the Irishmen took the stone, saying, "By ----, let us carry it over to Ireland."

Mrs. Murray set off to return to Aros by a different route, via Ach-na-Craig, and it was here at the inn that "Mr, and Mrs. MacLachan greeted her. 'Are you, Madam, the Mrs. Murray who has written a book of the Beauties of Scotland? Then you shall be welcome to the best horse I have, and may keep him as long as you please.' See what an advantage it is to have written a book!"

On July 31st she set off for the Ross of Mull and Iona, a journey of forty miles. It was a rough hot journey, made worse by taking the wrong track, so that she had to scramble for two miles up a zig-zag track. "The people in Mull jocosely say of their miles that they make up in measure what their roads want in quality!" She carried her own provisions and luggage." On the pommel of my saddle hung a bag containing drawing implements, in which I had brought 3 or 4 biscuits from Aros. In a small mahogany case containing hartshorn and lavender, a cure for bruises. I had some wine, also a tumbler, glass, spoon, knife and fork." After ten hours riding, partly along the side of Loch

Scridain, she at last found hospitality at Mrs. M'lean of Penny Cross. "'Madam, you being a stranger is sufficient reason for me to pay you every attention in my power, I beg you will come in'....I longed for a draught of porter....a bottle was brought in, and as it was a cordial to my drooping frame, Mrs. M'lean said, 'Have no fears, drink it all, I will tell no tales.'"

Mrs. Murray's interest in geology is seen again when she reached the Ross of Mull, and was astonished by the change from volcanic rock to the red granite. On arriving on Iona she went by sea to Port-achuraich, where St. Columba landed, in order to see the marble quarry. "where vast cliffs of marble rise in irregular masses from the sea to a good height," and she collected three kinds of marble: "pure white, white veined with bright green, and a light gray or rather dove colour." She also collected pebbles - "beautifully marked, fine lapis, nephritious, jaspers; green mixed with red; serpentine stone, gray and other porphyrios; pure white marble, and many other rare stones.... I also found one small amethyst, but not a clear one."

She seemed amused at St. Columba's aversion to women. "Why did St. Columba erect a beautiful edifice called the Nunnery?" However, the women were banished to the island of Women, or Nuns' Island, while the building of the Nunnery was in progress, "lest their charms and allurements should, by rendering the men less industrious, impede the great work."

She mentions that part of the ground around the Cathedral "was planted with potatoes and other vegetables; the rest overrun with luxuriant weeds.... I was fighting with the stubborn wild plants (up to my waist) to get a sight of the ancient tombs." There is a great belief amongst the inhabitants of Iona "that the last person buried keeps watch around the burying ground, until another is interred, to whose spirit the office of guardian is immediately delivered up."

"The soil which in general is white light sand, on which the sun in a wet climate has an astonishing effect in point of quick vegetation." There were claims that ploughing, sowing and gathering were all done within six months. Sheep were forbidden because of the smallness of the island, but cattle were kept.

"While we were seated on the rocks, numbers of women and children came after us and, by degrees, some of the old ones crept from rock to rock, until they were close to us; the herdsmen and boys kept at a respectable distance, not that they had less curiosity, but were more bashful than the women. The manner of the females appeared to me to be innocent, simple and crouching, like a spaniel dog approaching its master. If fear had not deterred them, I verily believe the poor things would have gladly fondled us. Very seldom indeed are their eyes accustomed to look upon a stranger of either sex. The clothes of the men and women were chiefly made of a thin coarse cloth which they fabricate, and dye of indigo colour blue....generally a petticoat, and a sort of bedgown of that cloth and a white mob cap or a handkerchief wrapped closely round their heads and under their chins. The men wear waistcoats, and trousers of the same sort of cloth."

On leaving Iona Mrs. Murray's party travelled by sea along the southern coast of the Ross of Mull to Carsaig. "These arches seem as though formed by the chisel and in perfect symmetry, but far too sublime for human art to touch....the sea flows in at the South West arch, and passes out through the North East one, and vice-versa at ebb tide....the sea rolls with considerable noise through these rocks even in calm weather."

Further along the coast Mrs. Murray describes the Nun's Cave, "now a shelter for the cattle from the heat and snow containing near a hundred cattle....screening themselves from scorching rays of the sun, the filth they made deterred me from going to the head of it, where I was told I might see carving on the rocks, executed by the persecuted Nuns who, it is said, took shelter in the cave, when they were driven from Iona at the Reformation." She had a "terrible scramble over slippery rocks to land, in order to enter it, and after all I was much disgusted with it," though she did comment that it would hold "300 armed men at a time."

Travelling on to Lochbuy she was impressed by the "vista of grand mountains on each side of the lake leading to the head of it (Lochbuy) where stands....the ancient Castle of Moy, near which is an excellent modern house (the same that Johnson and Boswell stayed at) surrounded by trees, and backed by the stupendous mountain of Ben Buy." She was given hospitality by Mr. and Mrs. M'lean Lochbuy and their numerous children. "Mrs. M'lean told me that to her knowledge the scenery at the head of Loch Buy had never been delineated by anyone but a carpenter while the new house was building....she showed me the carpenter's sketch....the idea that the beauties of Moy had never been delineated but by a carpenter, sharpened my pencil's petty talent. I also thought it a pity that such scenery should exist, and remain unknown. I therefore on the spot took up my pencil; I drew five different views....and in all of them I inserted the old castle."

She asked about serpents in the area and Mrs. M'lean replied "Aye." "She said archly, 'the rock on which you have been sitting is a nest of them.'" Later, "Loch Buy led me to the hold over the dungeon, it made my blood run cold to look at it....culprits were let down by ropes, and over the apperture a huge flat stone was laid."

On returning to Ach-na-Craig "where the cattle bred in Mull are embarked for sale in the South (of England)", while looking over the cliff face she had a most unfortunate loss. "I dropped out of my portfolio a cargo of wild flowers and leaves, collected on Mull, Iona and Staffa."

She also stayed on Ulva for a whole month because it was so often "unheeded by gentlemen of taste and mineralogical science because of lack of time. The Dowager Lady of the Late M'Donald Esq. of Boisdale, and her three daughters....so well informed....it required an effort to set myself at liberty....out of twenty-six days, only one was sufficiently fair for us to trust ourselves on the boisterous Atlantic near that island of Staffa, but so greatly was I amused at Ulva House, that I do not remember twenty-six days ever seemed to me to pass so quickly.... I scrambled amongst the huge fragments seeking fossils....amongst basaltic pillars, about 2 miles from the house on the South side. Bags, pockets, and even the skirts of our gowns, were filled with crystals of zeolite porphyry and spars."

She visited a cottage where the "fabric was divided into two appartments, one for the kitchen, the other for a bedroom, each being in size 6 or 8 feet square....no furniture....but stone seats, milk utensils, and an iron pot. In the bedroom was a chest or a small bed, the tester of which was the heath roof." Mrs M'Donald "acted the part of a Mother by all her sons people in Ulva....she is the life and soul of these parts, and crowds are daily at Ulva House, petitioning for comfort and relief both for body and mind.... There are very few good tradesmen inhabiting the Hebrides, because no man makes a single trade his sole study, but necessity often obliges him to be a shoemaker, tailor, carpenter, smith, in short a jack of all trades." She watched and described the fulling of cloth. "A great number of women are placed about a long table in a barn, whereon they spread the cloth, and then violently rub it with their hands, and sometimes their naked feet, see-sawing their bodies to songs appropriate to their work. It seems to be a most joyous scene, the fullers themselves being in the highest glee and animating each other with their vocal music till they get their highest pitch of the exertion and then they labour and sing through the day, and at night dance away their fatigue.... What effects the Gaelic music has upon Highlanders, when rowing, grinding, fulling or at any laborious work....what effect, too, has the bagpipes had on Highlanders in the field of battle."

View of the summit of Staffa from the area of the Clamshell Cove, showing the little islet of the Herdsman from a different angle, and also the cattle and their herdsman on the grass above the basalt columns.

A very dramatic view of the Carsaig Arches, which Mrs. Murray commented upon as she passed along the southern part of the Ross of Mull.

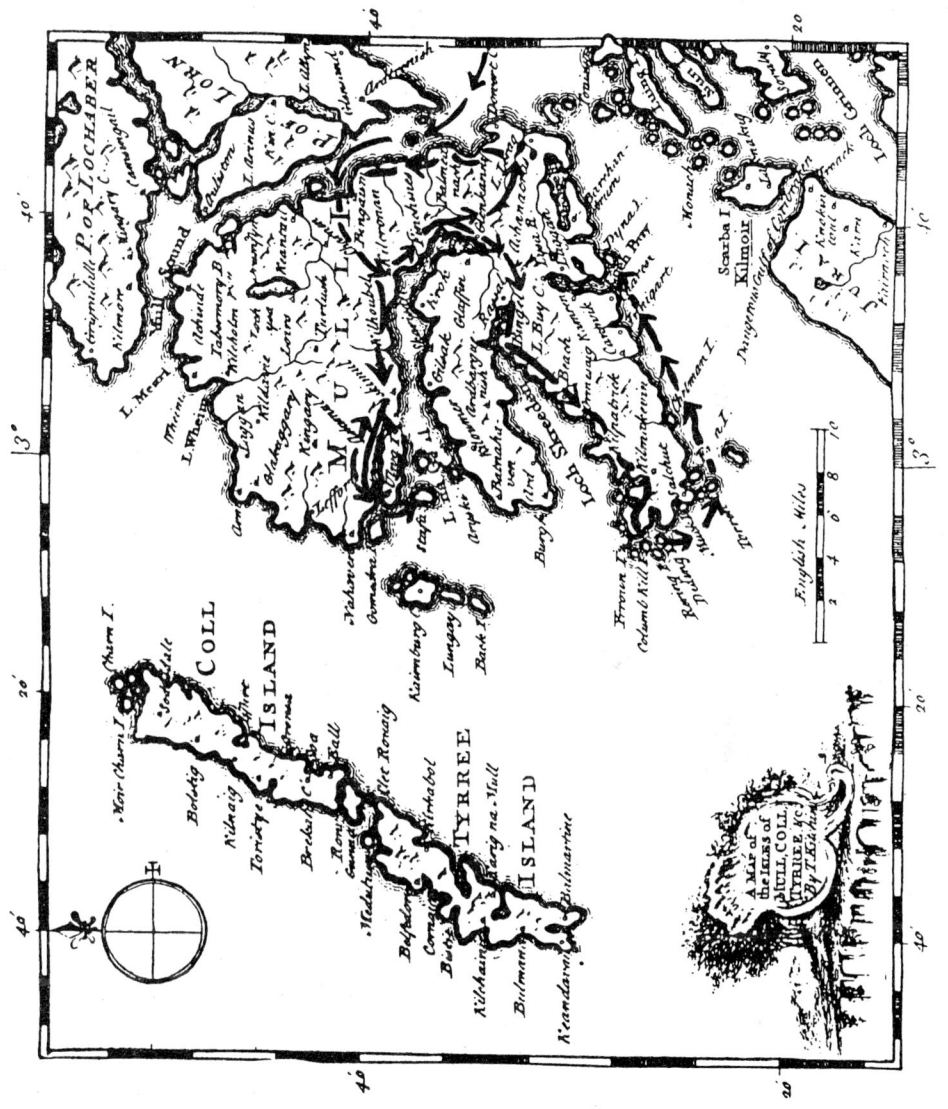

A map of Mull, Coll and Tyree, as well as Iona, Staffa and the Treshnish Isles, published by Thomas Kitchen at the begining of the 19th. century. With the route taken by Mrs. Murray marked on it.

Dorothy Wordsworth 1803.

In 1803 Dorothy Wordsworth had a brief view of Mull from near Oban, which she recalled in her Recollections of a Tour made in Scotland in 1803. She and her brother William were travelling to Dunstaffnage Castle, by way of Dalmally and Loch Awe. Coleridge, who had been travelling with them, had unfortunately just had to leave them when they had their first view of Mull. Dorothy described the scene: "And beyond, with leagues of water between, our eyes settled upon the island of Mull, a high mountain green in the sunshine and overcast with clouds, an object as writing to the fancy, as the evening sky is in the west, and though of a terrestial green, almost as visionary. We saw that it was an island of the sea, but we were unaquainted with its name; it was of a gem-like colour, and as soft as the sky."

Perhaps it was this view, so aptly described, which was to draw William back, to explore not only Mull but also Iona and Staffa, thirty years later, when he toured with his brother John and Crabbe Robinson. In any case, a number of poems resulted from the journey in 1833.

Dorothy showed herself to be a great walker, and a most intrepid traveller. They experienced some very frightening moments and great difficulties with their horse during their journey. The horse had to be forced into ferry boats or made to swim behind the boat. On one occasion he "beat with such force against the boat's side that we were afraid he should send his feet through (the side of the boat)."

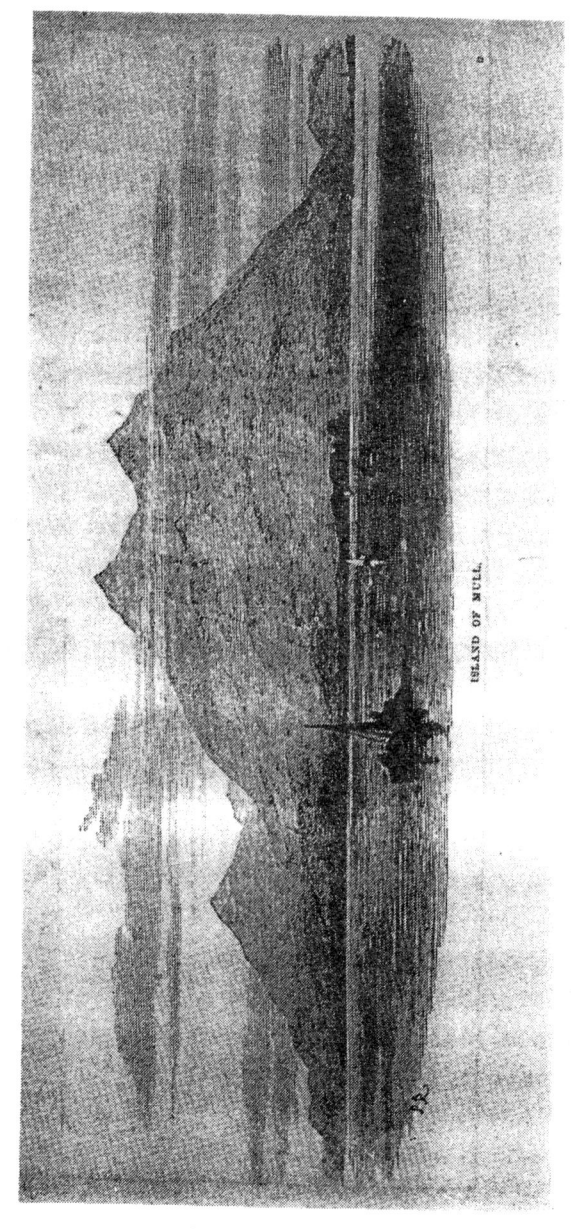

A print of the Sound of Mull, and the isle of Mull with the mountains "green in the sunshine and overcast with clouds", just as Dorothy Wordsworth would have seen it in 1803.

Sir Walter Scott 1810/1814.

Sir Walter Scott visited Mull on two occasions. On his first visit he sailed to Mull in a yacht of the Lighthouse Commissioners, and in 1814 he had just made a tour of the Orkneys and the Shetland isles before coming to the Hebrides. He kept a journal similar to that of James Boswell. And it was said by Lochart, who wrote in his Memoirs (Vol 4 Ch. 33), "We have before us, according to the scene and occasion, the poet, the antiquarian, the magistrate, the planter and the agriculturalist."

On one visit he stayed at Torloisk and, like many others before him, he received the usual kind hospitality from the Maclean family, and it seems that he was to some extent instrumental in bringing about a marriage in the family. His friend, Spencer John Alwyne Compton, heir to the Marquis of Northampton, accompanied him on this visit and later married Miss Marion Maclean-Clephane.

Scott loved the grandeur and isolation of the Highlands and Islands, and expressed this vividly in his poem <u>The Lord Of The Isles</u>, in which there are references to Staffa, Mull and the Castles in Morven:

> "The shores of Mull on the Eastward lay
> And Ulva dark and Colonsay
> And all the group of islets gay
> That guard famed Staffa round.
> Then all unknown its columns rose
> Where dark and undisturbed repose
> The cormorant had found
> And the shy seal had quiet home

And weltered in that wonderous dome
Where as to shame the temples deck'd
By skill of early architect
Nature herself, it seem'd would raise
A Minster to her maker's praise
Not for a meaner use ascend
Her columns, or her arches bend
Nor of a theme less solemn tells
That mighty surge that ebbs and swells
And still, between each awful pause,
From the high vault an echo draws."

Morag, the nurse who looked after Edith, the heroine, within the walls of Ardtonish Castle,

"Led her to where a turret airey head
Slender and steep and battled round
O'erlooked dark Mull! The mighty Sound
Where thwarted tides with mingled roar
Part thy swarth hills from Morven's shore
'Daughter,' she said, 'these seas behold
Round twice a hundred islands roll'd
From Hirt* that hears the Northern road
To the Green Islays fertile shore
Or mainland turn, where many a power
Each on its own dark cape reclined
From where Mingarry - sternly placed
O'er awes the woodland and the waste
To where Dunstaffnage hears the raging
Of Connal with his rocks engaging.'"

*Hirt - St. Kilda

In the notes by J. Logie Robertson which accompany Scott's Poetic Works (1834), he comments that "the Sound of Mull which divides Mull from Scotland, is one of the most striking scenes which the Hebrides affords the traveller. Sailing from Oban to Aros or Tobermory through a narrow Channel, yet deep enough for large vessels, on the left bord the mountainous shore of Mull with those of Argylshire, called Morven successfully indented by deep sealochs running many miles inland. To the south/east arise a prodigious range of mountains amongst which Ben Cruchan is pre-eminent, and on the north/east the not less huge picturesque range of Ardnamurchan hills. Many ruinous castles overhang the ocean. Those of Donolly and Dunstaffnage are just passed then that of Duart, then Ardtonish, Aros on the opposite shore then lastly Mingary. Spectacular rough passage and dangerous....so many inland lakes and gusts of wind, so that sublime sensations excited by the scene, that feeling of dignity, arouses from a sense of danger."

In the 1834 Poetic Works there are several vignettes of Staffa and the Western Coast which were done by W. M. Turner and engraved by E. Goodall. Turner stayed with Scott at his home at Abbotsford, and they planned these illustrations together.

Mingary Castle. One of the dramatic castles, overlooking the Sound of Mull, which feature in Sir Walter Scott's The Lord of The Isles. Here seen as an engraving c.1800.

Torloisk House (referred to as a Castle here) much as it would have been when Sir Walter Scott stayed in 1814. The ha-ha or low wall was built to keep the cattle away from the house, but yet to be invisible from the building, so that there should be a totally uninterrupted view from the first floor windows. In this case there is a wonderful view out to the isles of Ulva, Gometra and Staffa.

William Daniell 1815.

William Daniell, member of the Royal Academy, was principally known as an engraver. His accurate sketches were greatly admired by his fellow R.As, and when, in 1825, he and John Constable competed for the one place available for full membership, Daniell defeated the now much more widely known and famous painter.

At fourteen, Daniell was apprenticed to his uncle, Thomas Daniell, who took him on a tour of India, which included the Himalayas and the Southern part of India as well as Ceylon, making drawings and paintings of the mountains and temples which were later published for the expanding market interest in India at the time.

After that long tour, the idea of a journey around the coast of Britain cannot have seemed so very adventurous; in fact at one time he had considered rowing around the whole of Great Britain. However, stories of shipwrecks on the Cornish coast dissuaded him from this method of travel. He set off in 1813 to sketch the varied scenery around the coastline. Travelling by sea was becoming fashionable and Daniell thought that there would be sufficient travellers to subscribe to his publication A Voyage Round Great Britain. It took him ten years, having studied 4650 miles of coast and made many drawings. He produced 308 aquatints in 8 Volumes. He spent nearly six months in the Western Isles during 1815, which was fortunately a long fine summer. He felt that Scotland had not been "worthily dealt with by pencil." Although he followed the footsteps of Dr. Johnson, he was critical of Johnson's lack of feeling for scenery. Daniell was helped in planning his route by Sir Walter

Scott, to whom he dedicated the third volume of <u>A Voyage Round Great Britain</u>.

Daniell commented on some of the previous engravings of scenes in the Western Isles, which he considered misleading. He said of Staffa: "The spot seemed more worthy of attention, because those graphic delineations of it, which have obtained most circulation, are now found to be inadequate to the subject, and in many aspects utterly erroneous." This comment may have been applied to the engravings made after Mr Pennant's tour from drawings made by his servant Moses Griffiths "which have been so carelessly copied in several publications on the Continent, that the various objects have been reversed in their position."

Thomas Sutton in his book on Daniell says that, "William writes a complete guide to the Island of Staffa, including a full description of Fingal's Cave, and the unclean habits of the cormorants." Daniell's stay on Staffa resulted in a series of fine plates, which he himself thought of so highly that he had a special separate issue made, besides including them in his main work. Certainly the twenty odd plates which were the result of the six months spent in the islands are extremely dramatic and give a more realistic depiction of the island scenery than earlier drawings, which tended to try and make the views too romantic and picturesque. Daniell's study of the main street in Tobermory shows the Post Office, which was in Daniell's time the Custom House. Various other houses can still be identified today if you stand on the Ledaig Bridge and look along the main street as Daniell did a century and a half ago (see cover).

A print of Iona from the North East, showing the ruined Abbey as it was in 1815 when William Daniell made his tour and recorded over twenty views of the Western Isles.

Sir Charles Lyell. 1817.

Sir Charles Lyell, the well known geologist and president of the Geologists' Society, was also author of the Principles of Geology. A friend and correspondent of Charles Darwin, he wrote and worked during a time when many changes and advances were taking place in the world of geology. He was particularly respected for his ability to accept new theories and to change his own ideas when he saw that new discoveries made alterations to previously held opinions necessary. "When it was shown (by Darwin) that causes were at work which slowly and gradually modified the characteristics of plants and animals, so that they became adjusted to a self-adapting process to the changing circumstances around them, he adopted this view." (From Life of Sir Charles Lyell Vol 1 and 3.) In a tribute to Sir Charles after his death it was said that, "Perhaps the most striking characteristic was his remarkable mental plasticity.... This was nowhere more strikingly seen than in his change of attitude towards the great question of the Origin of Species, after the publication of Mr. Darwin's epoch-making work....it was the advancement of the philosophy of geology, not the advancement of self that he was constantly seeking."

Sir Charles' Principles of Geology prepared the way for Darwin's Origin of Species and Lyell supported and advised Darwin, as we can see from a letter dated 1836, in which he advised greater explanation in certain places of one of Darwin's papers and concluded, "Don't accept any official scientific place, if you can avoid it, and tell no one that I gave you this advice.... I fought against being president of the Royal Society as long as I could....the question is whether the time annihilated by learned bodies is balanced by any good work they do."

However, it was as a young man in the Autumn of 1817 that Lyell and two Oxford friends, Sir James Ramsey and Corbett, made a tour of Scotland including the Grampians and the West coast area, taking in Mull and Staffa. Following this he wrote a report for his father, which showed that Staffa's basalt formation had had a considerable influence upon the young undergraduate; and his description of the rise and fall of the waves on their boat while within Fingal's Cave makes one feel that you are there in the boat with them. "All representation of Staffa must fall short in expressing the bold and regular swell or semicircle in which the pillars are ranged on each side (of) the entrance. In a front view this, of course, is foreshortened and becomes nearly a flat wall. When we had walked in as far as we could by climbing along the side we returned to the boat and enjoyed a much more delightful view of it from the water. Fortunately the wind was Northerly and the waves were exhausting themselves on the other side of the island, which must otherwise have prevented us from getting in. When we had just passed the entrance a large swelling wave sucked us in suddenly a considerable way, the boat sinking at the same time five or six feet. There we were left motionless for some time and heard the wave slowly winding up the cave, and then dashing against the end of it. It then returned and carried us completely out again, raising us up at the same time.

The boatmen showed great address with their oars in preventing the boat from striking against the sides of the cave. After repeating this experiment several times one wave (I suppose a *Ninth*) threw us back so suddenly we were afraid to try again; the boatmen, however, would have willingly gone in again.

The echo in the cave is very loud. We had no bagpiper,

unluckily. The roof is ornamented with broken tops of the pillars.

P.S. The fact that the cave has broken pillars in the roof is very important geologically because it means it cannot have been formed by the action of the sea wearing away a plug of softer rock."

He also sent his Father the following poem recalling his impressions:

"Beneath the depths unseen of Oceans flood
While towered their heads on high, amid the passing cloud
And she had fashioned with an artist's pride
The dark black rock where hung the sparkling foam,
And many a step along its sculptured side
Had hewn, as if to tempt some foot to roam,
Some favoured foot of Mortal yet to come.
She bade no shapes of Terror there abound,
That pillar'd hall no guardian dragons' home,
But Ocean rolled his mighty waves around
To guard from vulgar gaze her fair enchanted ground."

From Lyell we learn something about the Boat Cave, which few of the other travellers mention at all... 'The pillars are ranged in a fine swell on each side, instead of being straight in the manner of a wall. With the beauty of Buachaille (The Herdsman, the small islet close to Fingal's Cave) and the cliff, we were astonished and delighted.....It was late when we landed at Iona, but the landlord of the Inn and his family had not returned from shearing. We were obliged therefore to go into....as miserable a specimen of a sheiling (shepherds hut) as can be imagined, a conical hut open at the top, with a large fire on the ground in the middle of the floor. Round the walls above us were immense stores of dried fish, tied two by two, and slung over a rope;... The whole was dirty in the extreme...the smoke our great enemy, being as dreadful as ever.....To avoid this, and relieve my eyes I walked out. It was moonblight and the finest aurora borealis I ever witnessed was lighting up the East. The ruins of the Abbey appeared to great advantage...Sir James got a bed at the schoolmasters, and Corbett and I slept at the Inn.

Sept 20th. The children crowded round us in the morning, with Icolmkill pebbles to sell. They are Serpentine, which they find on the beach, very unctous to the touch, and yellow. (Sir George Head in his Home Tour 1841 also mentions this custom). The schoolmaster, McLean, showed us the antiquities..... There are two fine crosses standing seven or eight feet high, of which there were once 360 standing. They were all thrown down at the time of the Reformation. The coltsfoot flourishes most magnificiently over the tombs, and hides much of the rubbish and treasures...The 450 islanders seem to exist by their fishing. Their only traffic is in kelp, and a few black cattle which they rear. We saw some black cattle embarked, which was a very amusing and ridiculous scene. A rope is tied to the horn of the animal, and he is driven to the seaside. At first they make violent resistance, and the driver while they are kicking and prancing yields with the rope, and lets them exhaust themselves, as an angler does a large trout. They show great dexterity in always keeping in front of the animal. The beasts are then pulled into the sea, into which both men and women walk...as if they were by nature amphibious. The forelegs of the animal are then lifted up by one person on each side, and then the hind, we saw one lassie sieze hold of the tail, and help to lift him in that way.....Having paid an enormous bill for our entertainment, we set off...determined to get back to Oban by passing along the South of Mull...this South-west end of Mull is a coast of red granite, and in McLeod's Bay, it takes a decided columnar shape, the pillars being four-sided whereas most of those at Staffa, which we examined were pentagonal, none square'.

Clamshell Cove, with visitors standing on the almost horizontal basalt columns.

John Keats 1818

The Poet John Keats and his friend, Charles Armitage Brown, visited Mull in 1818. They were making a tour of the northern part of Great Britain. Even before reaching Mull their journey had not been easy, as they had had to walk fifteen miles in the pouring rain in order to reach Oban, where they were upset to find that they were likely to be charged seven guineas for the trip to Staffa, which was their intended destination. Keats felt that this was an extortionate amount to be charged, and they planned to continue on to Fort William in the morning. However, as a letter to his brother Tom explains, later that same night the man who had spoken to him earlier about the journey to Staffa returned and said "what a pity it was we should turn aside and not see the curiosities, so we had a talk and finally agreed that he should be our guide across the Isle of Mull - we set out, crossed two ferries, one to the little isle of Kerrera of little distance the other from Kerrera to Mull 9 miles across - we did it in forty minutes with a fine breeze - The road through the island, or rather track, is the most dreary you can think of - between dreary mountains - over bog and rock and river with our breeches tucked up and our stockings in hand." They must have landed at Grasspoint, the closest point on Mull to the mainland and the landing and departure place, traditionally used for generations by travellers who wished to make the shortest sea crossing. It was from here that the cattle drovers conveyed their herds on their long journey South.

Their journey across Mull seems to have been by foot in continuing bad weather which Dr C.T. Andrews in the Keats-Shelley Bulletin (XXXVI 1975) feels was to some extent responsible for Keats' illness which led eventually to his early death from tuberculosis. They stayed the first night in a shepherds hut. "We had some white bread with us, made a good supper and slept in our clothes (which were no doubt damp) in some blankets....this morning we came about six miles and are now in, by comparison, a Mansion." (Derry-na-cullen on the map)

They would probably have had to spend yet another night getting to Fionnaphort, before they could set sail for Staffa. But once there Keats found their trials and tribulations had been all worth while as he wrote in his Poem <u>Staffa</u>:

> "Nor Aladdin magian
> Ever such a work began;
> Not the wizard of the Dee
> Ever such a dream could see;
> Not St. John, in Patmos' Isle
> In the passion of his toil,
> When he saw the churches seven,
> Golden-aisled, built up in heaven,
> Gazed such a rugged wonder,
> As I stood its roofing under.
> Lo! I saw one sleeping there,
> On the marble cold and bare;
> While the surges wash'd his feet,
> And his garments white did beat
> Drench'd about the sombre rocks;
> On his neck his well-grown locks,
> Lifted dry above the main,
> Were upon the curl again.
> 'What is this? and what art thou?'

Whisper'd I, and touch'd his brow;
'What art thou? and what is this?'
Whisper'd I, and stove to kiss
The spirit's hand, to wake his eyes;
Up he started in a trice:
'I am Lycidas,' said he,
'Fam'd in funeral minstrelsy
This was architectured thus
By great Oceanus!
Here his mighty waters play
Hollow organs all the day:
Here by turns, his dolphins all
Finny palmers, great and small
Come to pay devotion due -
Each a mouth of pearls must strew
Many a mortal of these days,
Dares to pass our sacred ways;
Dares to touch, audaciously,
This cathedral of the sea!
I have been the pontiff-priest,
Where the waters never rest,
Where a fledgy sea-bird choir
Soars for ever! Holy fire
I have hid from mortal man;
Proteus is my Sacristan!
But the dulled eye of mortal
Hath pass'd beyond the rocky portal:
So for ever will I leave
Such a taint, and soon unweave
All the magic of the place.'
So saying, with a Spirit's glance
He dived."

In the original version of this poem Keats had an extra five lines, which were inserted just before the final two lines, so that Lycidas finishes his hymn of praise to Fingal's Cave, by stating just what Keats obviously felt very strongly:

> "'Tis now free to stupid face
> To cutters and to fashion boats,
> The great sea shall war it down
> For its fame shall not be blown
> At each farthing quadrille dance."

So even in the early part of the 19th century commercialism and tourism were coming under fire from those sensitive beings like Keats, and we shall see that William Wordsworth felt just the same in 1833. What, one wonders, would they make of today's masses travelling by boat and coach to Iona and Staffa?

In a letter which Charles Armitage Brown wrote to C. Wentworth Dilke dated 7th. August 1818 he mentioned that Keats' 'cold' had become worse, and two weeks after spending the night in the shepherds' hut, when they had arrived in Inverness a local doctor thought that Keats was "too thin and fevered to proceed with the tour." However, he recovered to a certain extent during his return journey to London, on board a Cromarty smack, but in September and December the sore throats and fevers had returned, and Keats only lived another three years. So it seems possible that Mull's bad weather in the Summer of 1818 may have contributed to his early death.

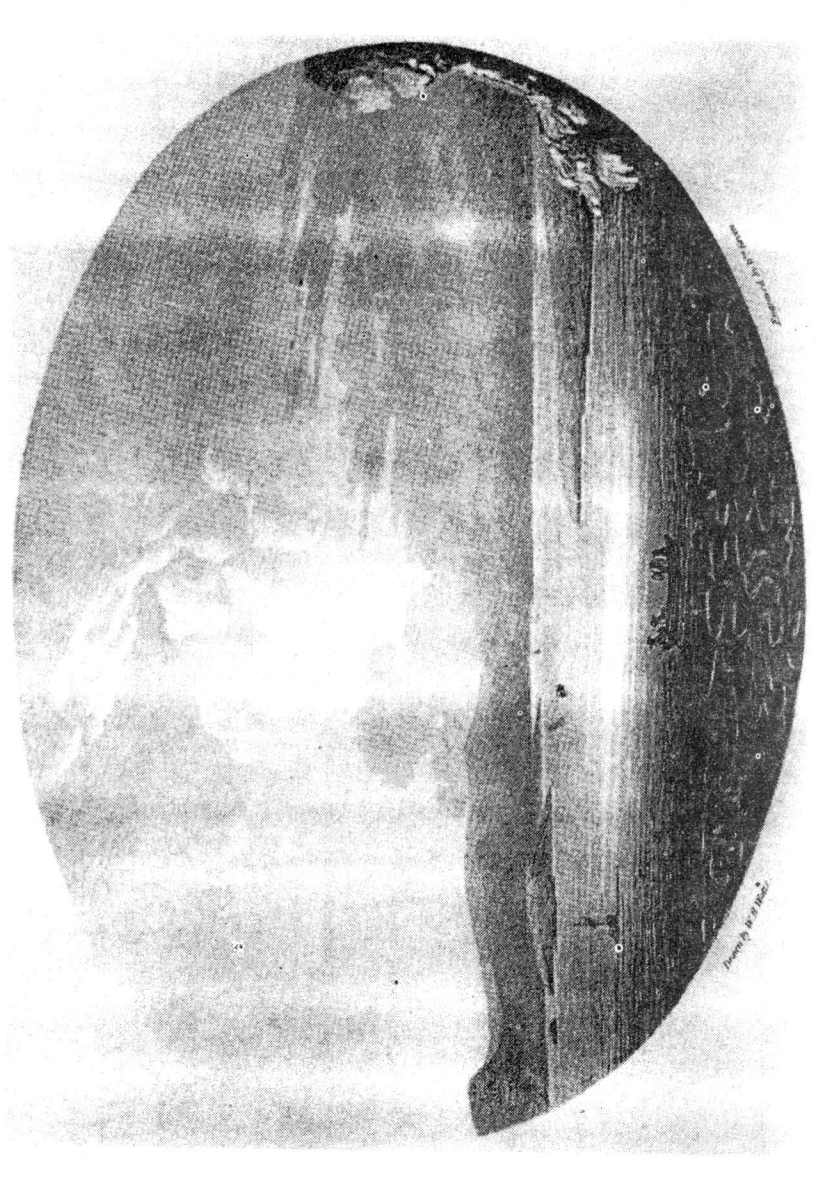

Passengers being ferried across the Sound to Mull, much as Keats would have been in 1818. In this early 19th. century print a horse is being taken across in the small open boat as well as the passengers.

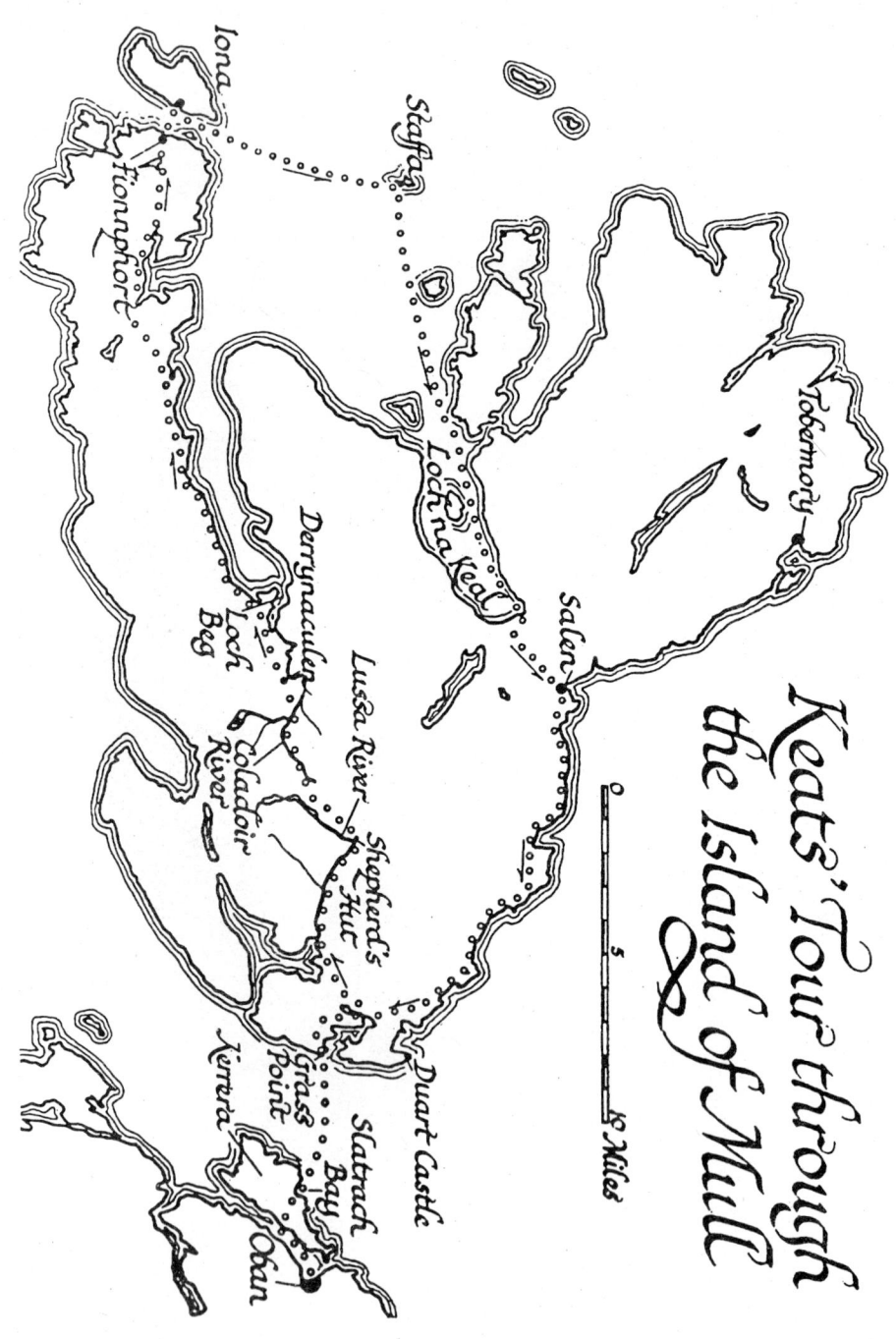

John Macculloch. 1824

John Macculloch, in a letter to his friend, Sir Walter Scott, gave a rather dour account of Mull, but it is never-the-less interesting because of his pertinent comments on the local traditional legends, and for its historical background.

"Mull is now as well-known as Edinburgh.... It is a detestable island, trackless and repulsive, rude and without beauty....rainy and dreary. Mull is a heap of rude mountains, almost every part of its shore is rocky or precipitous.... An accident happened on the top of Ben More....a hail-storm came on and in a few minutes the ground was covered. It became piercingly cold, though, in August; and one of the seamen produced some whisky in a tin cup. Being too strong for ordinary throats, I attempted to dilute it with hail; in an instant it turned so cold that I was obliged to drop it; the surface became covered with ice and it froze to the glass. This was a case of cold generated by the solution of the hail in the alcohol of the whisky, a fact before unknown....on pursuing the subject afterwards, in a correct manner, I found that the degree of cold this produced amounted to 39 degrees.... Tobermory....is disposed in a sort of cresent, containing some public buildings, and twenty or more slated houses....including a Customs House, an Inn, a Post Office, a Pier and some of the houses used for a cooper's store....a few boats are built here; but all the other business....which is trifling, depends on its Custom House, as it is the place where the legal forms connected with the herring fishery must be complied with....the difficulties of counteracting the habits of a people....the cause of its failure has been sought in the arrangements made for the new population that was enticed to it. The establishment included 2000 acres of land; an allotment was made to each house, at a low price.... Hence the idle, rather than the industrious flocked to it, while the want of ambition and industry, too characteristic of the Highlanders, combined with their agricultural habits, made them bestow on their lots of land the little labour which they were inclined to exert, neglecting the fisheries and manufactures which were the objects in the contemplation of the Society."

Macculloch visited Staffa and reported that there were now no less than twenty tour books which tell you "how you will be wetted, and wearied, and delayed, and frightened and starved and cheated, and disappointed, and drowned.... Once landed, the Great Cave may always be entered from above (from the Causeway) but as I am informed, it now requires a key.... It is with the morning sun only that the great face of Staffa can be seen in perfection, as the general surface is undulating and uneven, great masses of light and shadow are thus produced....in direct light (it) appears a flat insipid mass or straight wall.... As I sat on one of the columns (in the mouth of Fingal's Cave) the long swell massed the water at intervals up to my feet and in subsiding again left me suspended high above it; the silence of these movements and the apparently undisturbed surface of the sea caused the whole of the Cave to feel like a ship heaving on a seaway."

"The Treshnish Isles, consisting of Fladda, Lunga, Bach and the two Cairnburgs, form a chain to the Westward of Staffa; but except to a geologist, they are not interesting. I have had occasion to name the two Cairnburgs before as a seat of a castle in Norwegian times, or as having been falsely supposed by Pennant (to be) the limit between the Sudereys and Norderøys (The southerly and northerly groups of Hebridean islands). But there are now no trace of ancient works on it.... In 1715 it was garrisoned by the Macleans, and was taken and re-taken more than once during the Rebellion. It had been attacked before by Cromwell's troops, and here, it was fancied, were the rescued books from Iona burnt. There is a barracks on the smaller island which is still reasonably entire. On the larger, there are remains of a wall, with embrassures, skirting the cliff."

On visiting Iona he discovered that the famous Black Stones were no longer to be found and even the Celtic stone crosses of which he had heard so much were reduced from the "sixty or three-hundred and sixty" which he had heard mentioned in accounts. He is very dismissive of two local traditional legends, maintaining that the tales of Boethius (an early historian) are "encumbered with anachronisms. He reports that Fergus the 2nd brought away from the plunder of Rome by Alaric, whom he assisted, a chest of books and that he deposited these at Iona. Thus the present must have been made to a Monastery that had no existence, as the sack of Rome preceded the landing of St. Columba by more than a century. It took place in A.D.412 and Iona was not founded till A.D.563....and it is doubtful that he could have been at Rome in A.D.412, when he died in A.D.506." He is equally damning about the custom of Mercheta Mulierum, referred to by Dr. Johnson, again blaming Boethius. "The parent of all lies is the father of the Scottish Mercheta; it was established by King Evenus, who never existed, and the Scots submitted to it for a thousand years till it was formerly abolished by Malcolm the 3rd.... The Highlanders pretended that it was a power actually exerted by the Lord of the Isles."

Felix Mendelssohn. 1829

Felix Mendelssohn and his friend, Karl Klingermann, made a tour of Scotland in the Summer of 1829. At that time Scotland was considered to be the epitome of romanticism, and an essential part of any young man's education, particularly if he were of an artistic nature. So the two travellers made their way via Edinburgh and the Highlands to Fort William and Oban and thence to Tobermory. They experienced bad weather but the impact of Fingal's Cave was immediate, and despite seasickness and a rough sea, Mendelssohn started to compose the beginning part of the <u>Hebridean Overture</u>. This was to go through several alterations before the final version, but the main theme came to Mendelssohn while actually within Fingal's Cave. According to Ferdinand Hiller, a pianist whom Felix had met and corresponded with for many years, during the evening which followed their visit to the Cave, the two men were entertained by a Scots family who had a piano; but because it was Sunday it was not normally allowed to be played. However, after a great deal of persuasion Felix was able to just try out the first vital musical phrase.

During their travels Felix had done several sketches and in a letter he reported that he had "invented a new method of drawing (because of the weather) and have rubbed in clouds today and painted grey mountains with my pencil.... I finish my sketches during the rain." He made drawings of the Trossachs and also of the river at Killiecrankie, but he was obviously too busy composing while on Staffa to make a sketch. Klingermann was not so overcome by the grandeur of Fingal's Cave and reported that it was like "a monstrous organ. Black resounding and utterly without purpose."

It is interesting to know that Felix and Karl had made a diversion on their way to Edinburgh in order to see Sir Walter Scott at his home in Abbotsford. Felix and his sister Fanny had read many of Scott's novels and were admirers of his works. Unfortunately, having given no prior warning of their intended visit, they arrived just as Scott was about to set out himself, and consequently was not in the most receptive mood in which to stop and talk to two young Germans, whose accent probably made conversation difficult; and after all their trouble and extra travel, Felix wrote they had "half an hour of inconsequential conversation....we were out of humour with great men, with ourselves, with the world, with everything. A bad day." So even great men do not always get on as well as one might suppose!

Part of Mendelssohn's <u>Hebridean Overture</u>, which was inspired initially by his visit to Staffa.

A German engraving of Fingal's Cave from the begining of the 19th. century, with extremely regimented and orderly columns making the interior appear too neat and tidy, so that a great deal of the grandeur seems lost by being tidied away.

William Mallord Turner R.A 1831

When Turner was staying with Sir Walter Scott in 1831 at Scott's house, Abbotsford, in the Borders of Scotland, they were working on a scheme for Turner to illustrate Scott's poems. Probably Turner became intrigued by the descriptions of the Western Isles which he read in Scott's poems and decided to visit the area himself. He sailed first to Skye and then to Mull, where he took the steamship to Staffa. From 1820 regular sailings were available to travellers, so that one could travel either from Glasgow or Oban. Unfortunately for Turner, the weather was very bad once he had reached Staffa, and he only had an hour in which to scramble over the rocks to Fingal's Cave.

In a letter to John Lennox, who later purchased Turner's large painting of Staffa: Fingal's Cave, Turner wrote: "Such a rainy and bad-looking night coming on, a vote was proposed to the passengers: 'Iona at all hazards, or back to Tobermory?' The majority against proceeding. To allay the displeased, the Captain promised to steam three times around the island in the last trip. The sun, getting towards the horizon, burst through the rain cloud, angry, and for wind; and so it proved, for we were driven for shelter into Loch Ulver (Tuath) and did not get back to Tobermory before midnight." However, somehow Turner did manage to make a drawing of the inside of Fingal's Cave, the sketch for the vignette Fingal's Cave from the Inside which accompanies Scott's Poetic Works 1834, which is now in the British Museum Collection. There is some controversy about the position of the sun in this vignette, as in the original there is no sun portrayed. However, Turner was extremely interested in

Brewster's Treatise written that very year on Halos and Related Phenomena, in which he describes the sun in terms which sound like an echo of Turner's interpretations. "When the air is charged with dry exhalations, the sun is sometimes as red as blood. When seen through watery vapours, he is shorn of his beams, but preserves his disc white and colourless." However, in the published version of the interior of Fingal's Cave the sun is shown low on the horizon, but as Fingal's Cave faces South, it would not be possible to see the nearly setting sun in the position that Turner had placed it; so we can only presume that it was to add extra drama to the romantic setting that prompted him to add it to the final version.

The large oil painting Staffa; Fingal's Cave was exhibited at the Royal Academy in 1832, and was later sold to a buyer in the United States of America, the first of Turner's paintings to go there. John Lennox, who purchased the painting without actually having seen it, was disappointed and expressed his dissatisfaction with regard to the fact that it was indistinct and lacked detail. Turner replied, "Tell him indistinctness is my forte." The art critic, Finberg, said of this painting that it was the first to show Turner's "uniformity of treatment which enforces the feeling of Nature's union of all the elements against the puny devices of man. The cliffs and sea on the left are run together in continous strokes of paint." (Finberg Vol.1)

When exhibited at the Royal Academy, the painting had with it the following lines from Sir Walter Scott's Lord of the Isles:

Canto IV. "Nor, of a theme less solemn tells,
That mighty surge that ebbs and swells,
And still, between each awful pause,
From the high vault an answer draws."

John Gage, in his book on Turner, comments on the fact that Turner in this oil painting had introduced "the rare phenomenon of the haloed sun, which had been of particular interest to Brewster." So it appears that both Brewster and Turner were fascinated by these natural and dramatic effects, and one researched them scientifically while the other experimented with their impact in painting.

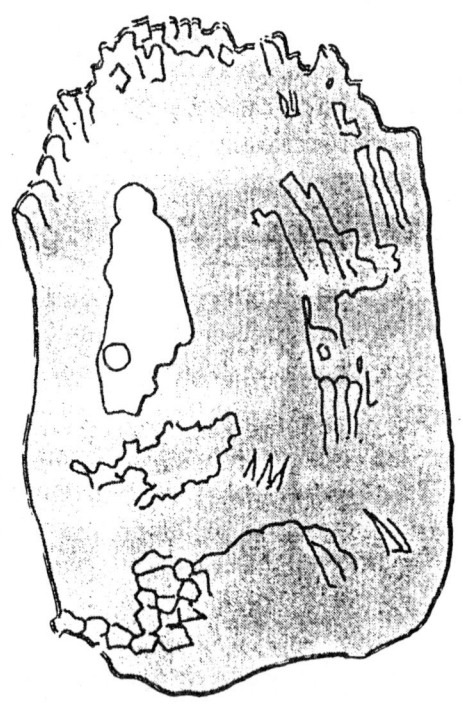

A sketch of Turner's vignette of the interior of Fingal's cave, showing the sun setting beyond the cave's mouth, an unlikely position, as is discussed in the text.

William Wordsworth 1833

William Wordsworth had first set eyes on Mull thirty years earlier, when he and his sister, Dorothy, had been on a long tour with their friend, Coleridge; but they had only a tempting view of the very green mountains soaring up into the sky, from the coast near Oban. Now in 1833 Wordsworth was a mature and established poet and, like Keats fifteen years earlier, he too found that the crowds of people who now flocked to both Iona and Staffa, partly because travel was so much easier, and partly because it was the fashionable thing to do, really disturbed his thoughts; so much so that he reports that "at the risk of incurring the reasonable displeasure of the master of the steamboat, I returned to the Cave and explored it under circumstances more favourable to those imaginative impressions, which it is so wonderfully fitted to make upon the mind." The result of this time spent alone in the Cave can be seen in Sonnet XXIX <u>Cave of Staffa After the crowd had Departed</u>:

"Thanks for the lessons of this Spot - fit school
For the presumptuous thoughts that would assign
Mechanic laws to agency divine;
........The pillared vestibule,
Expanded yet precise, the roof embowed,
Might seem designed to humble man, when proud
Of his best workmanship by plan and tool.
Down-bearing with his whole Atlantic weight
Of tide and tempest on the Structure's base
And flashing to that Structure's topmost height,
Ocean has proved its strength, and of its grace

In calms is conscious, finding for freight
Of softest music some responsive place."

Whereas when he was surrounded by the jostling crowds his feelings were rather different:

Sonnet XXVIII   <u>Cave of Staffa.</u>

"We saw; but surely, in the motley crowd,
Not one of us has felt the far-framed sight;
How could we feel it? Each the other's blight?
Hurried and hurrying, volatile and loud?
....

To be able to stand and 'Gazing take into his mind and heart,
With undistracted reverence, the effect
Of those proportions where the almighty hand
That made the worlds, the sovereign Architect
Has deigned to work as if with human Art?'"

Once out of the cave, Wordsworth was able to comment on the scenery: "Upon the head of the column which forms the front of the cave, rests a body of decomposed basaltic mater, which was richly decorated with that large bright flower the Ox-eyed daisy."
And he addressed the flowers on the top of the cliff:

"Ye fresh flowers that brave
What Summer here escapes not, the fierce wave,
And whole artillery of the western blast.
....But ye, bright flowers, on freize and architrave
Survive, and once again the Pile stands fast."

In all he wrote four sonnets on Staffa and four on Iona. One of the Iona sonnets recalls the oaths which were once sworn on the Black Stones. According to Martin Martin, "Macdonald, King of the Isles, delivered the rights of their land to his vassals in the Isles....with uplifted hands and bended knees, on the black stones....solemnly swore that he would never recall those rights which he then granted; and this was instead of his Great Seal."

> Wordsworth noted that the stones are actually grey in colour.
> "Black in the people's minds and words.
> Yet they were at that time as now, in colour grey.
> But what is colour, if upon the rack
> Of conscious souls are placed by deeds that lack
> Concord with Oaths?"

The local island children followed the party of visitors. Wordsworth deplored the way that they begged holding out

> "Wave worn pebbles, pleading on the shore,
> Where once came monk and nun with gentle stir,
> Blessings to give, news to ask, or suit prefer."

Although he found their method of making a few pennies unattractive and perhaps alien to his ideals of Iona, they were only taking advantage of their new-found source of wealth. Before there were visitors, there was no-one to beg from; so the visitors themselves had created the market.

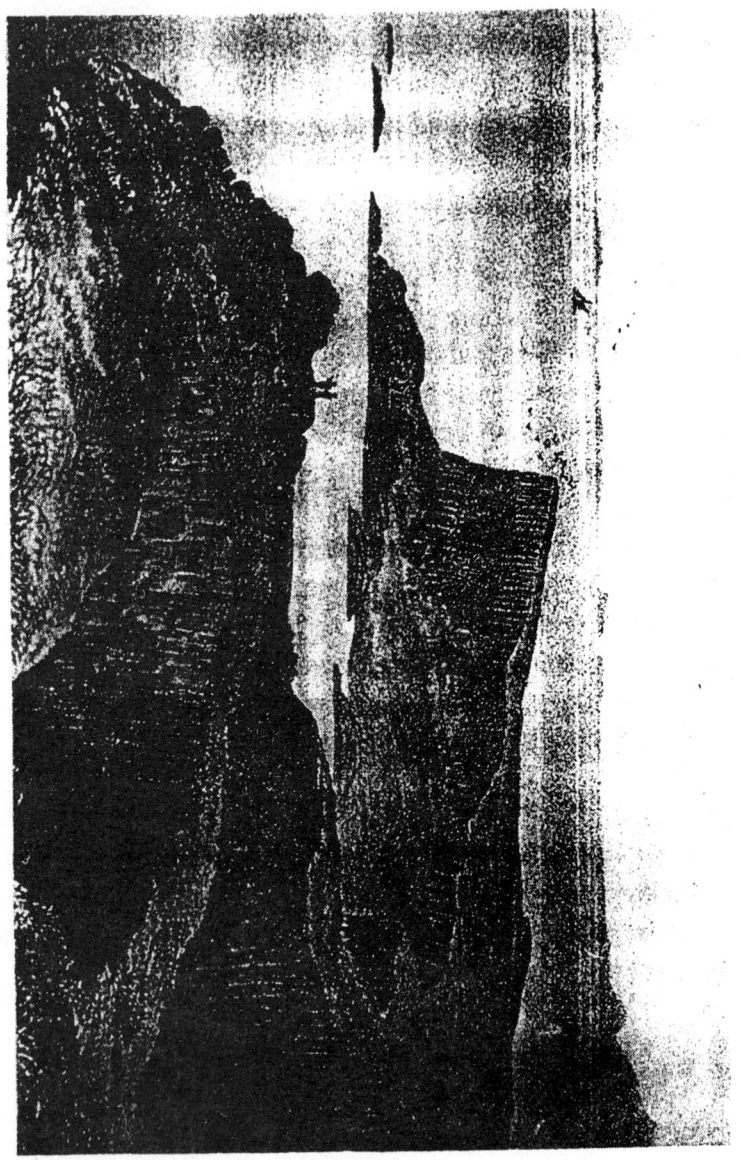

The summit of the Isle of Staffa, as it would have appeared to Wordsworth when he addressed the flowers on the top of the cliff.

Sir Robert Peel. 1837

Sir Robert Peel was the British statesman and prime minister during the 1840s, who carried the country through the difficult days of the Corn Laws and Catholic Emancipation, but who died as a result of an unfortunate accident while out riding in Hyde Park on a new horse, which threw Sir Robert, causing him to sustain very serious and fatal injuries.

It was while he was making a speech following his election as Rector of Glasgow University (although elected in 1836 this speech was not delivered until January 1837) that he spoke the famous lines:

"I have stood on the shore of Staffa, I have seen the majestic swell of the ocean, the pulsations of the great Atlantic beating in its inmost sanctuary and swelling a note of praise nobler far than any that ever pealed from human organ!"

This speech was made to a large audience of Scottish middle-class listeners who were not used to hearing an English ex-prime minister speak, but who were willing to pay as much as twenty-five shillings a head for that privilege. Sir Robert addressed his audience directly and personally, telling them of his hopes to see the Government progress forward and to throw off the corruption with which it had been branded and above all to see it "animating industry, encouraging production, rewarding toil, correcting what is irregular, purifying what is stagnant or corrupt." To use the image of Fingal's Cave, with all its power and might, was an interesting idea, which he obviously felt would be particularly relevant to his Scottish audience, and one which they would be sure to understand.

A French print of Staffa, giving a truly romantic but unrealistic view, so that it looks as though the whole island is being raised up by the force of the waves.

John Wilson 1841

A Voyage Around the Coast of Scotland and the Isles 1841.

John Wilson was requested by the Commissioners of the Board of Fisheries, to accompany their Secretary in the Summer of 1841 on an investigation into the natural history of the herring. On the 3rd. July their party anchored for the night off the sheltering shore of Ulva in Loch Tuath, on their way to Staffa and Iona. "We had a good view of Mrs. Maclean Clephane's residence, Torloisk, a capacious-looking mansion placed on a wide semi-circular inclined plain, surrounded by a considerable extent of young plantations and backed by mountains."

On arriving at Staffa they found another boat there. "We ere long found that she contained the guides, or rather the guardians of the island, who (were) required to visit Staffa that day to attend the debarkation from an expected steam boat....these guides really poison, by their pertinacious attendance, the tourist's very life in solemn places, and none like Staffa where there are such impressive features to be seen in silent wonder; surely the less that's 'said' the better." There was a building "intended as a place of refuge or refreshment for visitors....the tenant, we believe, pays about £20 a year rent for Staffa....we perceived two large ravens....afterwards informed that this felonious pair had not left alive a single lamb."

Later Wilson reported on the arrival of a "steamer with her motley crew and cargo of enthusiastic tourists....and although those great and un-respecting levellers, the ocean waves were heaving around with a howling wind....we could see the not-altogether undismayed indulgers in the picturesque, descending the vessels sides, then hovering in mid-air for a few brief moments of suspense, and finally and fearfully wedging themselves in the tossing boat.... One very tall columnar-looking thing in black was at first regarded as a spare funnel, but as it descended with the rest into the boat, and was observed to wear a white neck-cloth, we....concluded that it must have been a clergyman."

Despite his opinionated comments on his fellow men, he does give some details of the surroundings which were neglected by other travellers; "The weather was moist and dull" when they landed on Iona, where "a lengthened range of cottages faced the sea, with one small parliamentary church and a manse....the Duke (of Argyle)....has taken to constructing protecting walls (to the Abbey ruins) and accredited one or more natives to exercise a vigorous surveillance on all intruders, such as carry bags and hammers....a couple of years have not elapsed since a fingering knave of a mineralogist knocked off poor Abbot MacKinnon's nose; after this announcement of the wrong, we think he will scarcely venture to show his face with it in public."

Wilson noticed that on Iona they "met the country people in decent, well-dressed knots....a sprinklings of blythe company on their way to a service. Wilson and his party were "under the necessity of clearing the Sound before the turn of the tide," so did not attend the service themselves. In any case, as Wilson pointed out, they "might not, perhaps, have made much of the Gaelic sermon at any rate."

He and his party passed the Skerry-vore Lighthouse "which lies about twelve miles out in the Atlantic, south-westwards of the Island of Tiree. Many a fair vessel and gallant crew have been lost upon its insidious and scarce seen ledges: but this death in darkness is now being converted under the superintendence of Mr. Alan Stevenson, to a saving light, which will ere long cheer the heart of the belated or uncertain mariner as he approaches these dangerous outworks of the Western Isles, and guide him towards some assured haven. We got a good view through our glasses of its low abhorrent front, now crowned by a great uprising column of enduring granite (from Erraid); but although it was a beautiful morning, both calm and clear, there was yet a low broad heaving swell from the Atlantic, and the surge itself warned us not to land....and John Hill our trustworthy pilot, seeming very desirous to give the redoubtable Skerry-vore as wide a berth as was compatible with our indulging in a general view of its position and improvement, we speedily bore away for Tiree." They were given a drawing by Mr. Alan Stevenson (Robert Louis Stevenson's father), the resident engineer, of the building as it will appear after its completion, which will probably be effected in the course of the present summer."

A view of Clamshell Cove on Staffa, showing the type of small boat which travellers in the 18th and 19th. centuries depended on, to transport them to these remote islands.

Statistical Survey, Argyll 1843.

The Statistical report for Argyll for the year 1843 gives a very detailed survey of life and conditions on Mull, Coll and the other islands, setting out the rents paid by the proprietors of the various properties.

"There are eleven landed proprietors, whose names and valued rents in Sterling money are as under:

Hugh Maclean of Coll	£ 82 14 11
Mrs Clephane Maclean of Torloisk	£ 59 4 4
Francis Will Clark Esq of Ulva	£ 49 5 3
Hugh MacAskill Esq of Calgarry	£ 40 4 2
F. W. Caldwell Esq of Tobermory, and J. Stewart Esq of Achadashenaig, for Mishnish	£ 33 16 11
J. Stewart Esq of Achadashenaig	£ 6 16 10
Lachlan Macquarie Esq of Glenforsa	£ 27 15 2
British Society	£ 10 2 4
Misses Macdonald	£ 13 16 8
John Forman Esq W.S. Staffa	£ 2 9 2
Kenneth Campbell Esq of Ardow	£ 2 17 3
Total rent	£329 3 0

Before the Reformation there were no less than eight places of worship in this parish (Kilninan and Kilmore), the ruins of which are still to be seen, although, after the Reformation, and down to the year 1827, only one clergyman was left to serve the cure; a lamentable want of spiritual instruction, therefore, necessarily existed, as, from the great extent of the parish and its numerous islands, it became impossible for the parishioners to attend, with anything like regularity, the parish church; and to any one clergyman, however zealous, serving the cure of a charge so extensive and divided, the duty became more than physical strength could perform. In the year 1827, the Parliamentary Commissioners, acting under the execution of the Acts 4 and 5 George IV, erected two parishes *quoad sacra* in this parish and planted a church in each.

The survey then goes on to mention the Antiquities in Kilnian: "On the height above Kilmore (Dervaig), there are five large stones disposed in a kind of circular form, and supposed to have been a place of worship in the times of Druidism. Cairnburgh or Cairnburg, one of the Treshnish isles, was anciently considered a place of great strength, and supposed to have been fortified in Norwegian times. It is a high rock, of some considerable extent on the top, and inaccessible on all sides, excepting by one narrow pass. In 1715 it was garrisoned by the Macleans, and was taken and retaken more than once during the rebellion of that year. It was attacked and taken by Cromwell's troops in the days of the Commonwealth; and here, it is fancied, were the rescued books from Iona burned. Little Carnburgh is a smaller rock near it, and separated by a narrow sound, to which the same description applies. These rocks are said to be the boundary of the two governments into which the Hebrides were divided when subject to the Crown of Denmark, called the Nodorees and the Soderees....and tradition bears that the two governments not unfrequently contended for the possession of this stronghold...."

"Mansion Houses.... Calgary Castle, the seat of Hugh MacAskill, Esq, is a neat modern building, and appears to considerable advantage from the sea. Torloisk, the beautiful seat of the late Mrs. Clephane Maclean, is situated amongst thriving plantations, and commands a fine view of the Ulva north loch, and the Treshnish islands."

"Industry....Agriculture. In agriculture, considerable improvement has been made since the last Statistical Survey, and there is a greater quantity of crops now produced, arising from the different system of management which now prevails, especially on farms of any extent....considerable quantity of wasteground brought under cultivation; and the cultivation of turnips and clover, formerly unknown in this corner, is now making rapid progress. The Cheviot sheep were some years ago introduced by Mr. Cameron, one of Mr. MacCaskill's tenants, and they are thriving beyond all expectation.

Formerly Kelp used to be manufactured on the different properties in this parish, which contributed considerably to the support of the population; but, of late years, this source has entirely failed, as no kelp is now made."

"Parochial Economy.... There are two churches, one at Kilnian and the other at Kilmore (Dervaig) at the distance of seven miles from each other. Both these churches were built in 1745, and are kept in tolerable repair. Last year they underwent a thorough repair. There are five schools in the parish; one the parochial school, another the General Assembly's and a third supported by the Society for Propagating Christian Knowledge, a fourth by the Gaelic School Society, and the fifth by the Glasgow Auxilliary."

The Survey also covers customs and legends. It would appear that a custom prevailed in this country, even as recently as forty years ago, of the inhabitants setting off to the hills with their flocks at the beginning of the summer, and bivouacking in the vicinity of the best upland pastures, "where all the families of the district took up their residence till it became necessary to descend to the low grounds in the month of August, when the hill pasture became bare, and their crops required attendance...." During the summer months the "men occasionally visited the low grounds to attend to their simple husbandry....or to procure some of the delicious fish which abound along the coast, some engaged in the chase, or followed the game; and richly did they deem themselves rewarded for their toil. When they returned to the family circle, the produce of the flocks and dairy were put before them, and the feast enlivened by the pure essence of mountain dew, joined to the heart-stirring strains of the bagpipe. Nor in this pastoral encampment were the women idle; much of their time was occupied in the labours of the dairy, in preparing an abundant stock of butter and cheese for winter. When 'baughting time' was over, the females used the distaff and spindle, and, congregating on the sunniest bank, enlivened the task of providing the tartan clothing for the family by the simple yet innocent strains of their mountain songs."

"Amongst the numerous islets and rocks which skirt the Ulva shores....on the shores of Ormaig is Christy's Rock, regarded by the people of Ulva with peculiar feelings, as being in olden times the scene of a melancholy drama.... An industrious woman, visiting her dairy one day, missed a kebbock, one of the fairest and best. Suspecting a young girl, she accused her of the theft. The maiden denied the charge, and pled innocent; but the guidwife, chagrined at her loss, and, in order to extort a confession, seized the girl, and wrapping a 'tonag' or plaid round her neck, dragged her to a small rock near the encampment, and let her down from the verge, with a view of extorting a confession, or deterring her from committing like depredation in future. Unfortunately, the tonag tightened, and strangulation took place.... The guidwife became inconsolable, for the girl was a near relative of the family....while her neighbours, collecting to the fatal spot, regarded her with the utmost abhorrence, as a murderess.... No formal trial took place to restrain the popular indignation. They bound her in a sack....carried her to the Ormaig shore, and there placed on a rock covered by the sea at high water, she slowly terminated existence by the rising tide. The rock still bears her name, and is the 'Sceair Caristina' or Christy's Rock before noticed."

"A private census taken in 1837" showed that "the island contained a population of 604 souls. In this population there are shoemakers, square-wrights, boat-carpenters, tailors, weavers, blacksmiths, drystone masons, and two merchants, all more or less engaged in agriculture. Each tenant has a boat, some two, this being as necessary an accompaniment of an island farm as the cart to a low country farm. The boat is in never-ending requisition, the using it for fishing being only one of the many purposes it serves. In seed time, it collects the wreck (wrack) and manure, and in harvest time takes home the grain, potatoes, and the peats; in a word, next to his horse it becomes, in the management of his farm, the islander's right-hand."

"Along the Ulva shores shell-fish of every description are to be found, including the oyster and clam, lobsters, crabs, spout-fish (razor-shell), limpets, whelks, etc. Skate, flounder, lythe, plaice, sole, turbot, seath, perch, mackerel and dog-fish, etc. are abundant; herring, cod, ling, girnot, etc. and large quantities of salmon have been found in the Ulva North Loch. There are also otters, seals, porpoises and most sea-fowl that are common on the west coast of Scotland, whether as natives of this district, or birds of passage, such as cormorants, scarts, teals, scale drakes (shell ducks), ducks of various kinds; and the migratory are swans, swallows, cuckoos, lapwings, woodcocks, solan geese, curlews, wigeons. besides these, eagles, hawks, kites and geese, wild pigeons, ptarmigans. Black cock, grouse, plover and snipes are to be found, and rabbits and hares are abundant.

"When the celebrated Dr. Johnson visited this island (seventy years earlier) no plantations were to be seen. Wood, young trees and planting are now making great progress, and the room where the Doctor spent the night in Ulva, indulging his bile against the then unclothed appearance of the landscape, is yet to be seen in the old Macquarrie mansion house. The new mansion house is the seat of Mr. Clark....it is a large modern building and placed in an extensive park, about 400 yards distant from the old mansion-house of the ancient Macquarries, the earlier proprietors of these estates; the natural beauties of the grounds interspersed with thriving plantations; the splendid panoramic view of Ben More, and the other Mull mountains; and the Sound, with its green islands, all tend to create in the scenery around the mansion-house beauties of a peculiar and very high order. From the drawing-room windows of the mansion, looking towards Mrs. Clephane Maclean's and Mr. Clark's property in Mull, and about two miles to the north, is to be seen, on Laggan Ulva, the singular cataract of Erse-forse. A stream collected on the mountains seems to make way with impetuosity down the hillside, and describing in its tumbling course two minor waterfalls, it descends in an unbroken sheet from a precipice, 90 feet high, into the Ulva North Loch.

"The Ulva garden, containing about two acres, is well-stocked with every kind and variety of fruit, and so early are the productions that strawberries are ripe here as soon as that fruit appears in the Edinburgh market.... The Ulva church and manse, two neat and fine-looking buildings, erected in 1827, are distant about five minutes walk to the north of the mansion. Towards the Sounds, and beside the Ferry, are the Ulva Inn, smithy, merchant's shop, ferryman's and other houses. The Inn, during the last year, was put by Mr. Clark in an efficient state of repair, and a new innkeeper having taken the establishment, every accommodation can now be given to parties on pleasure trips coming to visit Staffa, and the scenery around, boats and men being at all times in readiness.

"The smaller island of Gometra, separated from Ulva by a very narrow channel, contained, by the annexed census taken in 1837, 168 souls, the soil and character of its products being nearly the same as Ulva. It has two harbours, the one facing the south, and the other the north.

"The still lesser island of Collonsa (Colonsay) has only a population of six souls. Staffa is uninhabited, and is about one mile long and a quarter of a mile broad.

"The people of Ulva are very healthy and capable of undergoing much fatigue. The language chiefly spoken is Gaelic, although there are few, if any, but can understand the English. The habits of many of the people are not over industrious. Their ordinary food is porridge and milk, potatoes and fish, sometimes varied with a little mutton or beef. Too much snuff and tobacco are used; and the females have of late been indulging in tea, which they readily get in exchange from the merchants for eggs. Very few instances occur of habitual inebriation. Taking them in mass, their general character as a people may be stated as shrewd and calculating; they are peaceably disposed and religiously inclined. All attend the parish church. There are four Dissenters in the parish, and one Roman Catholic.

Tobermory.

"The town of Tobermory, which is a thriving sea-port, encircles the extremity of a fine sheltered bay, and is one of the safest harbours among the western isles, being protected from the Sound of Mull by the small isle of Calve, which stretches nearly across the entrance but leaves ample room at its northern point for the largest vessels to enter the harbour, though none but the small craft can effect this at the south-east point, even at high water. The British Society for extending the Fisheries and improving the Sea Coast of the kingdom commenced the town in 1788; and so well has the village prospered that at that time there were only two houses where at present there is a population of nearly 1500. The British Society and Frederick William Caldwell, Esq. of Mishnish, are the proprietors of the village. The town is well built, and possesses two good quays. The new quay was begun in 1835 by the late Colonel Campbell, and is now nearly completed; it gives four feet at low water, being two feet deeper than the old quay. The former is a little to the north of the latter, and nearer to the entrance of the bay. The town has increased considerably on Mr. Caldwell's side of late years; and the harbour is much frequented, both by steamers and sailing vessels. The church, which was erected in 1827-28, stands in a fine prominent situation behind the principal part of the town, and overlooks the bay. There are at present two schools in operation in the village, one a government or parliamentary school, and attended, in the winter season, by about 100 scholars; and the other a school of industry for young females, attended by about 90 scholars, supported chiefly by the bounty of her Majesty Queen Adelaide. A Sabbath school is likewise kept, where about 200 boys and girls receive religious instruction; there is likewise a public reading room.

"In the sixteenth century, during the northern retreat of some ships forming part of the Spanish Armada one of the vessels, was blown up and destroyed off the harbour of Tobermory.... The timbers of this ship are still occasionally brought up. Part of the wood of this vessel was presented by Sir Walter Scott to his Majesty George IV, on his visit to Edinburgh. Several attempts were made to recover the sunk treasure: one in 1688, by Sacheverell, Governor of Man, who fitted up diving bells and tried them with success at the depth of ten fathoms. The report of the country goes that he got up and recovered much treasure. (Rather a different report from that of Sacheverell himself!) Another attempt was made in 1740 by Sir Archibald Grant and Captain Roe, to weigh her by means of divers and machinery. This attempt was unsuccessful, but some guns were brought up."

A panoramic view of the Main Street of Tobermory, showing the neat layout of the houses and the quay. Taken prior to 1828 and therefore not showing the church standing behind the town.

Queen Victoria.

Leaves from my Diary, Aug. 1847.

Having sailed from Osborne in the Isle of Wight and visited the Scilly Isles and Wales, they sailed up the West Coast of Scotland. The Queen arrived with Prince Albert, her brother Charles and her two eldest children, along with some friends. They "came into the Sound of Mull by Tobermory, a small place, prettily situated, and from then the views continued beautiful. At one o'clock we were in sight of the Isles of Rum, Eig and Muck (rather large islands which Lord Salisbury bought a few years ago). Next we passed the long flat curious Islands of Coll and Tiree, the inhabitants of these islands have unhappily been terrible sufferers during the last winter from famine (the famine which followed the potato blight). A little further on we saw to our right the Treshnish Isles, very curiously shaped rocks; one is called 'The Dutchman's Cap', the most strange shape thus:

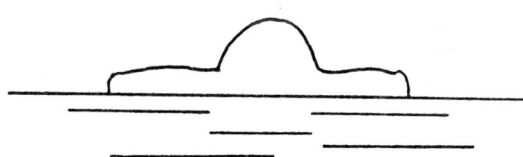

"At three we anchored close before Staffa and immediately got into the barge with Charles and the children and the rest of our people, and rowed towards the Cave. As we rounded the point the wonderful basaltic formation came in sight. The appearance it presents is most extraordinary; and when we turned the corner to go into the renowned Fingal's Cave, the effect was splendid, like a great entrance into a vaulted hall: it looked almost awful as we entered and the barge heaved up and down." Victoria was one of the few visitors to mention the colours in connection with the cave: "The rocks under water were all colours, pink, blue, green, which had the most wonderful effect." Three cheers were raised by the seamen, as it was the "first time the British Standard with a Queen of Great Britain and her husband and children had entered Fingal's Cave." They passed close by the Herdsman but then the swell that was rising drove her back to the yacht; she was a bad sailor as she often mentioned in the Diary. However, Albert and Charles, his brother-in-law, returned to Staffa before going on to Iona. "I and the ladies sketched;" they could see, "the ruins of the old Cathedral of St Oran and when Albert returned they said the ruins were very curious....fine old crosses and tombs of ancient kings were still to be seen. I must see it some other time." Did she really hope to return? Or was it the difficulty of disembarking gracefully, while wearing a crinoline, with no proper pier or landing stage, which lessened her interest?

"On Albert's return, we went on again and reached Tobermory at nine. The place was all illuminated." Next day, Fri. Aug. 20th, they rose at 7.30 and left Mull in pouring rain, so she "went down and drew and painted." Unfortunately she doesn't record in the Diary what the subject of those drawings was, and she left no sketch on Staffa, but we do have her delightful little record of the Dutchman's Cap.

The landing place on Iona, with the rough stone pier where visitors were disembarked, and the row of stone cottages which form the main street.

Alfred Lord Tennyson 1853

Alfred Tennyson visited the West Highlands with another poet, Francis Turner Palgrave, in 1853. There is no definite documentation that they travelled to Staffa but, taking into consideration the fact that Staffa and Iona were often the final destination for seekers after the Scottish romantic tradition, and considered to be the ultimate in places which inspired ideas, whether they were transcribed in poetry, music, or drawing and painting, it seems possible that Tennyson's poem Sea Dreams, could well have been influenced by a visit to Staffa.

"Then she told it having dream'd
Of that same coast. But round the north a light,
A belt it seemed, of luminous vapour lay
And ever in it a low musical note
Swelled up and died: and as it swell'd a ridge
Of breakers issued from the belt and still
Grew with the growing note and when the note
Had reache'd a thunderous fulness on these cliffs
Broke mixt with awful light (the same as that
Living within the belt) whereby she saw
That all those lines of cliff were cliffs no more
But huge Cathedral fronts of every age:
Grave, florid, stern as far as eye could see
One after one, and then the great ridge drew
Lessening to the lessening music, back
And past and into the belt and swell'd again
Slowly to music."

A description somewhat reminiscent of Queen Victoria's notes of her own experiences recorded in her Diary, written just years earlier, where one has the same feeling of being lifted up by the waves, before being dropped down again, only to have the whole sensation repeated over and over again.

A print of the interior of Fingal's Cave, showing the visitors in typical English dress of long coat and trousers. This is identical to another print of the cave on page 75, which shows the visitors in Highland dress.

Jules Verne 1859.

According to his nephew Maurice, the novelist Jules Verne had three main passions in life, which were; freedom, the sea and music; and as Verne himself put it, he "could not see a ship leave port, without his imagination setting sail as well." His visit to Scotland in 1859 included a West Coast cruise to the Hebrides. Here he was able to indulge the second of his passions, and he was so fascinated by the Isle of Staffa and the beauty of its sea caves that he incorporated the island with a genuine natural phenomenon, described by scientists and extolled by writers of romantic novels, and called the Green Ray. So he used these to provide a most unusual setting and basis for his next novel The Green Ray.

Helena, the heroine of this novel, The Green Ray, hears of the phenomenon, which under favourable conditions may be seen immediately the last vestige of the setting sun disappears behind a perfectly clear horizon; and even more importantly for this story, she learns that those who manage to glimpse this so-called "Living Light", will never be deceived in matters relating to the heart, and will be able to see clearly into their own heart, and be able to read the thoughts of others!

So accompanied by her two adoring twin uncles, she sets off for Oban, where the western horizon is usually clear and unobstructed, so that the Green Ray could usually be seen. Helena's admirer at this time is a dull character called Austobutus Ursidos, who believes that life is composed entirely of facts. (His creation apparently owes a great deal to Verne's admiration for Dickens and his character Mr. Gradgrind in Hard Times, who had no room in his life for romantic thoughts.) However, en route for Oban, Helena is involved in an incident in which she rescues a sailor, Oliver Sinclair, from the terrible whirlpool of Corrievrechan; and it is he who accompanies Helena and the uncles when they set off for Staffa and Iona, having been thwarted in their attempts to obtain a clear view of the horizon while they remained in Oban. So they are determined to set up camp, actually in the Clamshell Cave on the isle of Staffa itself.

Verne's description gives a vivid impression of Fingal's Cave and the angularity of the rocks: "There ranged in order were hundreds of prismatic columns of equal height, as if produced by some gigantic process of crystalization, their cut sides standing out as sharply as though they had been chiselled by a sculptor. The external angles of the one adapting themselves geometrically to the internal angles of the other, some had three sides, some four, and even a few up to seven or eight, which gave some variety to the general uniformity of the style and proves the artistic order of nature."

According to Verne's story, Helena is 'over attracted' by the strange romance of the place and allows herself to be lost in a day-dream while in Fingal's Cave. At that moment a severe storm blows up, so that she is trapped inside; Oliver goes to her rescue, and while performing this incredibly brave act in a small boat, gets carried into the already storm-bound cave. The boat is immediately smashed to smithereens on the columns at the end of the cave. However, Oliver manages to grab a projecting rock and finds Helena; they cling together, sitting in Fingal's Armchair (a seat-shaped recess right at the rear of the cave) throughout the night. They amazingly survive this incredible and unlikely ordeal, despite the fact that Helena swoons away in Oliver's arms. The next morning the storm abates and the tide ebbs, so they are able to escape from the cave, to the amazement of the uncles and friends who had given them up for lost. That day the horizon is completely clear and while the twin brothers watch and wait they recite alternately verses of their beloved Ossian (the poet whose work had been 'discovered' and was being hailed by some as the greatest discovery of Scottish poetry ever made. However, others cast grave doubts on the authenticity of the poet and the verse). The twins are successful in seeing the Green Ray, but Helena and Oliver glance at each other at the precise moment and so miss seeing the phenomenon. But "Helena has caught the black ray shining from the young man's eyes, and Oliver the blue ray shining from hers." So the story has a happy ending.

Oban harbour with early steam ships and paddle-steamers as well as sailing boats. Oban would have looked very like this when Jules Verne visited in 1859.

William Black (author of Macleod of Dare 1879).

William Black, the Victorian Romantic novelist, and the author of The Princess of Thule set his very long 3 volume novel Macleod of Dare in the southern part of Mull. The story starts as young Macleod of Dare, the 6th son of Lady Macleod, is given a traditional send-off on his journey from Mull to London by a piper. On the boat to the mainland young Dare gives a poor woman and her children his plaid to keep them warm. "That was the way of the Macleod's of Dare, they had a royal manner with them; perhaps this was the reason that their revenues were now far from royal."

When he arrives in London in June, he is struck by the "change from the sombre shores of Loch-Na-Keal, Loch Tuath and Loch Scridain, to this world of sunlit foliage." He is entranced by a young beautiful actress, Gertrude, and they spend a day on the river Thames. He asks himself if she is not Fionghal, the Fair Stranger who, as Hebridean legend goes, came across the seas to the dark shores of the isles. But he is uneasy when he sees her being a 'coquette' on the stage. She is looking for a husband who would not prevent her from continuing her acting career. In order to keep up appearances, Macleod entertains her in an extravagant manner, which he can ill afford to do.

In the Autumn he returns to Mull, and is at first glad to be back, but his character has changed and he dismisses a trusted servant and sends him back to his home to the Isle of Gometra. He no longer hunts deer or grouse but urges all his servants to hunt otters, in order to have the skins made up into a fur coat for Gertrude. When a long letter arrives from Gertrude, his cousin Janet, to whom he has confessed his longing to return to London, suggests that he could make the purchase of a grain drier, the excuse for going south again. Once there he declares his love for Gertrude, despite being very upset at seeing her in a worthless play. She asks for a week in which to decide, at the end of which she agrees to marry Macleod. He returns to Mull to tell his mother that Gertrude will arrive next year; his mother feels that Castle Dare is too shabby for entertaining, and he then announces that Gertrude will become his wife.

When, at the start of Volume 3, Gertrude arrives with her father, they are traditionally welcomed by the bagpiper; but instead of enjoying the music, she shows her dislike of the sound, and also complains of the cold. Hamish, an old retainer, said, "A fool would he be that would burn his harp for her" (see Garnett). After a stormy night and day, the following evening was fine with a full moon, and Hamish suggested a boat trip to Iona. Gertrude and her father were not at all keen but were persuaded to set out. At first it was extremely beautiful with phosphorus stars on the waves, but then another storm blew up and they were soaked; however, they managed to land on Iona at Martyrs' Bay, and walked across the island. But Gertrude saw only desolation and fell very silent, while near the Abbey ruins she was frightened by the jackdaws. Macleod showed her the graves of his ancestors and signified to her that he wished to be buried on the Treshnish Isles. At that moment a black lamb rubbed itself against Gertrude's legs and she fainted; on her recovery she asked her father to take her away; he agreed and said, "You are not fitted for this savage life....the Hebrides seem scarcely in the world at all....the sea cuts you off from everything you know."

Gertrude feared she would be forgotten by London theatregoers, and that her face would be burnt by the sea air and the sun, which would also spoil the portrait she was having painted by Lemmel in London. Shortly after this she broke off her engagement and returned to London. Macleod was a broken man when he heard she was to marry her portrait-painter, Lemmel. Hamish upbraided Macleod for being so weak and proposed that they should carry Gertrude off from the wedding ceremony before she was married. The kidnapping of Gertrude was successful, but once on board the boat for Mull, she begged to be put ashore and refused to eat or drink. Once again a storm blew up and as they neared their destination, they were warned that

> "As you pass through Jura's Sound,
> Bend your course by Scarba's shore
> Shun, shun, the gulf profound
> Where Corrieveckan's surges roar!"

Gertrude and Christine, her companion, were put ashore with Hamish, when they reached Mull, but Macleod was drowned, and one is reminded of his ill-fated wish to be buried on the Treshnish Isles.

So ended this highly improbable and romantic tale, which gave such a gloomy picture of life on Mull in contrast to the bright lights of London, and stressed Gertrude's very different values to those of Macleod, and calls attention to the prophesy "Fool is he that burns his harp for her."

An interior view of the ruined Abbey at Iona, with foliage growing on the walls. Jackdaws would probably have nested and roosted in this greenery, when Gertrude made her unhappy visit!

Robert Louis Stevenson. 1885

Robert Louis Stevenson spent many years of his boyhood on the isle of Erraid, just off the Ross of Mull. His father was the engineer in charge of the building of the Dhu Heartach lighthouse at Skerrievore. The rock for the lighthouse was intricately cut in the quarries at Erraid before being shipped out to the Dhu Heartach Reef to be assembled rather like a jig-saw.

The island had a lasting effect on Stevenson, as he said in an essay entitled <u>Memoirs of an Islet</u> which was part of his book <u>Memories and Portraits</u>. In this he speaks of artists and writers who "use, time after time, the matter of their recollections, setting and resetting little coloured memories of men and scenes.... After a dozen services in various tales, the little sun-bright pictures of the past shall shine in the mind's eye, with not a lineament defaced, nor a tine impaired." He used two islands in particular in just this way, "the little sandy isle in <u>Allan Water</u>" and the isle of Erraid, of which he said:

"There is another isle in my collection, the memory of which besieges me. I put a whole family there in one of my tales: and later on, threw upon its shores and condemned to several days of rain and shellfish on its tumbled boulders, the hero of another (David Balfour in <u>Kidnapped</u>).... I am under a spell to write of that island again.... The little isle of Erraid lies close to the south west corner of the Ross of Mull: the Sound of Iona on one side, across which you may see the isle and the church of Columba; the open sea to the other."

The first tale he referred to was that of <u>The Merrymen</u>, a story that deserves to be better known, and of which Mr. Ridley says in the introduction, which he wrote to one edition of <u>The Merry-</u>

men, that it contained "some superb pieces of description and a magnificent climax. Until (Stevenson) wrote The Weir of Hermiston Stevenson hardly achieved anything more powerful than the last paragraph. But the tale as a whole is of unsatisfactory length, too long to be a short story, and hardly enough material in it to be a short novel. But it was one of Stevenson's favourites and he was an exacting critic of his own work."

The tale itself may have been based partly on a combination of myth and history, combining as it does the traditional mythical tale of the sea kelpie or mermaid, and the stories of seals that speak, presaging terrible disasters and the historical event of the famous Spanish wreck in Tobermory Bay. The story is told in the first person, which gives added drama to the whole thing, and Stevenson gives his uncle in the story a totally unreasonable fear of the 'great feesh', which he believes follows his small boat. The house in which he lived was full of strange pieces of furniture salvaged from a wrecked ship; this makes his daughter Mary Ellen very uneasy. It transpires that the uncle has murdered one of the survivors from the last wreck and is haunted by what he has done!

Stevenson vividly tells of yet another storm blowing up: "There had begun to arise out of the south west a huge solid continent of scowling cloud; here and there through rents in the contexture, the sun still poured a sheaf of spreading rays; and here and there, from all its edges, vast and inky streamers lay forth along the yet unclouded sky. The menace was express and imminent. Even as I gazed, the sun was blotted out." Uncle and nephew watched the next ship, which is doomed to death upon the Merrymen. A group of terrible rocks, around which the sea, in calm weather, creates "a little dancing mutter of sound as though the Roost was talking to itself. But when the tide begins to run again, no man could take a boat within half a mile of it, nor a ship afloat that could steer or live in such a place. You can hear the roaring of it six miles away. At the seaward end there comes the strongest of the bubble; and it's here that the big breakers dance together the dance-of-death, it may be called that have got them the name in these parts of the Merrymen.... I have heard it said that they run 50 feet high, but that must be the green water only, for the spray runs twice as high as that. Whether they got the name from the movements which are swift....or from the shouting they make about the turning of the tide, so that all Erraid shakes with it, is more than I can tell."

It is an exciting and dramatic story, which ends with the discovery of a black man, who appears to have survived the shipwreck, and this finally drives the uncle completely mad. After an ill-conceived plan to get the stranger to accept food and shelter, he runs off to his death. The final paragraph of the story shows Stevenson's effective and dramatic narration: "My uncle Gordon saw in what direction, horrible to him, the chase was driving him. He doubled, darting to right and left; but high as the fever ran in his veins, the black was still swifter. Turn where he would, he was still forestalled, still driven toward the scene of his crime. Suddenly he began to shriek aloud, so that the coast re-echoed; and now both I and Rorie were calling to the black to stop. But all was in vain, for it was written otherwise. The pursuer still ran, the chase still sped before him screaming; they avoided the grave and skimmed close past the lumber of the wreck; in a breath, they had cleared the sand, and still my kinsman did not pause, but dashed straight into the surf; and the black, now almost within reach, still followed swiftly behind him. Rorie and I both stopped, for the thing was now beyond the hands of men, and these were decrees of God that came to pass before our eyes. There was never a sharper ending. On that steep beach they were beyond their depth at a bound; neither could swim; the black rose once for a moment with a throttling cry; but the current had them, racing seaward, and if ever they came up again, which God alone can tell, it would be ten minutes after, at the far end of Aros Roost, where the sea birds hover fishing."

The second tale Stevenson referred to was, of course, the far better known story of <u>Kidnapped</u>, David Balfour's Journey in 1751. In this case Stevenson "threw upon its (Erraid's) shore" the hero, David, and he, not being used to the sea and tides, failed to realize that, although he had been marooned on the island, he could, at low tide, wade ashore quite easily. It was only after several days, when some Gaelic fishermen laughed at his plight and explained the tides to him, that he was able to escape, having survived on shellfish. He reached the Ross of Mull and thence began his journey along the Ross, passed Ben More to Torosay. A journey of fifty miles as the crow flies, but longer for David Balfour because he lost his way and had many adventures.

Stevenson was also well-known for the famous <u>Skye Boat Song</u>.

> "Mull was astern, Rum on the port,
> Eigg on the Starboard bow;
> Glory of youth glowed in his soul,
> Where is that glory now?"

So we can see that he certainly did "use time after time....the little coloured memories of men and scenes."

The Dhu Heartach Lighthouse, built by Stevenson's father, on the rocks at Skerrievore.

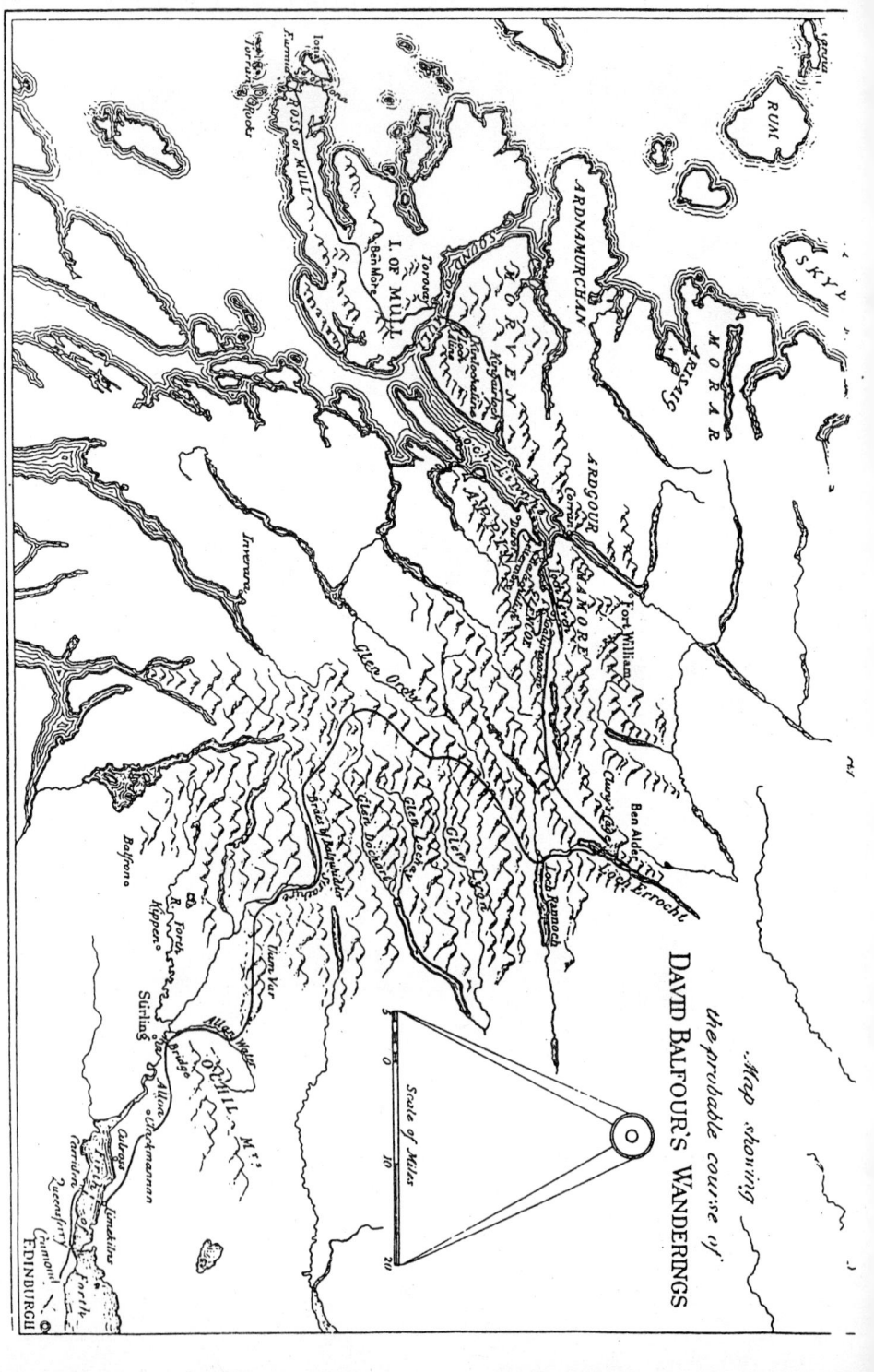

Angela Du Maurier 1937-1950.

Angela Du Maurier, Daphne's sister, stayed at Torosay Castle at various times between 1938-1945, as a guest of the Guthries'. And in her autobiography It's Only The Sister, she explains her love for Mull rather than for Skye.

"Skye is beautiful but so grim and foreboding, that there is not found that beatitude which is found on Mull.
Mull with her silver birches, oaks, rowans.
Mull with her larches and fir trees.
Mull whose Ben More, Sguu Dearg, Ben Buie and Dun Na Ghaoithe are every bit as fine as the Cuillins, but so much kinder:
Mull with her Duart and Lochbuie; her fairy glens and glades through Torosay and Ardura. And whose Great Glen in its own serene beauty is one more Road to the Isles."

"It was the treelessness of Skye that gave me that strange unfriendly feeling, the treelessness and barren serenity of the Black Cuillins themselves."

In 1938 Olive Guthrie, who owned Torosay at the time, invited her to stay. She needed help with the rhododendrons, which were threatening to take over the gardens! So Angela was invited into a life of "duck shooting in the dusk, stalking (which had me winded before I'd climbed half a mile), scraping mussels off rocks for evening dinner's *moules marinières,* and sawing rhododendron branches by the hour!"

"The wild beauty of Mull in October is indescribable. The birches have turned golden and the oaks and beeches a firey red;

there are rowans bright with scarlet fruit at every turn, and as dusk fades into night and you stand on the doorstep....there comes the low thrilling sound of the stags' roar in the forest.... Then the full moon, the 'hunter's moon', appears in the sky and from Torosay you can pick out clearly by its light the outline of distant peaks, and across the gleaming bay, the untouched stately walls of Duart, the oldest inhabited castle in the land. All is still....then perhaps a heron calls....it is cold....and you turn and go inside to a peat fire."

While at Torosay in 1939 she finished her novel The Spinning Wheel, which used Mull (under a disguised name) as its background. In 1940 she spent nearly the whole year in Mull. Strings of Convoys passed daily in the Sound; it was a very secret area and Angela had to have a special green identity card and all mail to the island was censored. Because of her French name, she was very nearly expelled but managed to persuade the local policeman that her brother was fighting for Britain, and that her books *were* in the Oban Library, and so established a reputable identity.

"My own life was now a curiously split one mentally. Part of me was naturally with the various members of my family, but most of me was in Mull where for what it was, I gardened with Olive alone in the grounds, which had in the past boasted eight or ten men, and now had one boy. Winter was setting in and it was bitterly cold, because naturally, wartime restrictions made many fires or central heating and even baths impossible. We used to wrap rugs round ourselves in the dining-room in the evenings and I remember quite well going to sleep under four blankets, an eiderdown, a fur rug, four hot water bottles, wearing flannel pyjamas, a cardigan and a woollen rug.... Cold it may have been, but an exquisite dry cold with snow on the mountains and frost on the trees snow-thick. Olive's eldest grandson, David James, arrived bearded, off his M.T.B. for Christmas Day for his twenty-first birthday, and on Boxing Day with most of his relations home on leave, a shoot was organised."

During the Summer of 1941 she finished another novel <u>Trevergan</u>, finding Mull an excellent place for writing. "I worked harder on <u>Trevergan</u> than I had on the others, harder, that is to say, at the time of writing. I put in eight hours a day for two months and I finished it. Mull was the perfect place for writing, I had always found it so. Olive and the children left me in complete peace, seeing me at meals and in the evenings. Sometimes I wrote, if fine, on a small balcony with its view of terraced gardens, the bay, Duart and Cruchan in the distance, and later when it was cold (or if it rained) in the dust-sheeted drawing room...." She fell more and more under the spell of Mull and, finding a farm at Achnacroish for sale, she bought it, hoping to renovate it and live there herself, but wartime legislation preventing "individuals from spending more than an infinitesimal amount on property....ruled my dreams out of existence!

"I yearned more than ever for the time when the little house of my dreams should be mine. Achnacroish, the small farm now empty and disused, which lay below the little cairn just inside the deer-fenced forest, ten minutes up the hill from Torosay, alone in the glory of its highland solitude. Here I knew I would one day do good work. And to Achnacroish I daily made my way.... Instead of painters, builders and carpenters, the sorry scene was a mere replica of the last act of Tchekov's <u>The Cherry Orchard</u>, as one by one the boards were nailed to the windows. But day by day, week by week, month by month and year by year I waited.... In the autumn I made my annual dash Mullwards; this time a mere two weeks had to suffice, and it was this time (Autumn 1941) I think that enemy planes swooped over Torosay and dropped their bombs on ships off Oban....a convoy, killing some valuable horses, which were being sent overseas, the well known crump crump of falling bombs sound singularly out of place in the stillness of the night."

Olive Guthrie died in the Summer of 1945, and Angela returned for the funeral. "I arrived on Torosay beach to hear in the distance a lament being played on the bagpipes. Then out of the teeming rain came mourners so numerous that one could not count them.... Olive was laid to rest beside Murray, her husband, under the massive granite cross which stands in splendid isolation on Torosay's most Eastern shore, looking forever to Loch Linnhe, Ben Nevis, and the rising sun."

In the post-war years of 1950 Angela still hoped to return to what she most wanted, "that small low cottage at Ardnacroish." But it was not to be.

Although not so well-known as her sister Daphne, Angela was a writer to whom a sense of place, in this case Mull rather than Cornwall, was of equal importance for the background to her novels, and it is sad that she did not fulfill her dream to live in her cottage at Ardnacroish.

Torosay Castle looking much as it would have done while Angela du Maurier was a visitor, between 1937-1950.

The Mitford Family 1930/1940s

The Mitford family spent a good deal of time on holiday in their house on the isle of Inch Kenneth. Lady Redesdale obviously loved the solitude and the contrast with life in London, even if she did still have her library books sent up, and had a Harrods order regularly delivered.

The six talented sisters - Nancy, Diana, Pamela, Jessica, Deborah and Unity - all accompanied their mother on visits to Inch Kenneth, although they did not all enjoy the life up there as much as Lady Redesdale, as the following excerpt shows:

"The journey to Inch Kenneth was grim; it was impossible to get up there in a day from Paris. I elected to spend a night in Glasgow; the great attraction there was the picture gallery with the Burrell collection. Next morning there was a train to Oban which caught the boat to Mull. At Salen, Muv's ancient shabby car would be waiting; there was a drive of eleven miles across Mull and then a mile of sea to Inch Kenneth in her boat, *The Puffin*. One arrived half-dead to a wonderful welcome and a delicious Scotch tea.

As Muv grew older one of us took her up to Scotland when she left London every April. Once she and I arrived at Oban on a stormy day and when we disembarked at Salen Pier there was no car; this meant that it was too rough for her boatman to be able to cross from Inch Kenneth to Mull. With our mountains of luggage we went to the inn, but it was full. We sat on plastic chairs in the bar, tired out. Muv was completely unmoved but the thought that we should be sitting there for the rest of the afternoon, and for the unnaturally light evening, and then all night long, and possibly for several days until the weather changed, sent my heart into my boots. It was all I could do to conceal my despair. There was no question of going back to Oban; Muv would never have dreamed of such a thing and in any case there was no boat until the following day. The rumour soon went round the village that Muv was marooned, and a saintly old person appeared with an offer of putting us up for the night. I slept badly; it was the uncertainty that was so depressing. There was no particular reason why the storm should abate. Late on the following day the old motor appeared; we had only been twenty-four hours at Salen but it seemed like a fortnight.

"We crossed to Inch Kenneth on a grey and choppy sea. Clambering from the dinghy into the motor boat, both of them dancing on the waves, was not easy for Muv, aged eighty, but as we settled into the stern of *The Puffin* wrapped in oilskins against the driving rain, she shouted to me above the horrible noisy wind: 'Fun, isn't it?' I shouted back, 'Great fun.'

"I never quite understood the love my mother felt for her island. It was inconvenient to the last degree. There was no telephone, and if the sea was rough there was no post. She spent a good deal of each day looking through field glasses to see if any people should chance to appear on the opposite shore at Gribun, or whether a black spot had been fixed on her garage which meant there was a telegram for the island. When, on a calm day, the boat went over to fetch the mail, excitement mounted. Ages seemed to go by, even after the boat came back, until the little sack was given to Muv to open. If it contained nothing but bills the disappointment was dreadful.

"When I was going to the island, Debo (Deborah) started writing a week in advance, and wrote every day, so that I could be sure of a letter from the little sack; I did the same for her. It sometimes seemed as if the post which linked her to life and to the mainland was far and away Muv's greatest pleasure, a close second being the wireless news and the newspapers.

"It was difficult not to wonder whether the trouble and annoyance of the long journey were worth while if, at the end of it, one was to live for letters and news which were so much more readily available almost anywhere else. However, I kept these impious thoughts to myself, and the island had compensations in its lonely beauty. If Muv saw through her binoculars that there was a picnic party on Mull, or better still if a yacht appeared in the Sound, she sent her boatman to fetch whoever it might be and then gave them a terrific tea. She said during the time it took for the boat to make the journey, her cook had time to make fresh scones. There again, such a haphazard choice of guests was, to me, a strange taste. It must have been the gambler in Muv which made her positively enjoy the unpredictable journeys and the luck of the draw at her tea parties."

Jessica, in her autobiography A Fine Old Conflict, tells of the chance circumstances of the purchase of Inch Kenneth, and how, despite her father's intentions to cut her out of his will (because of her marriage and her political views) she became the owner of one-sixth of the island. She thought it would be an amusing joke to donate her share to the Communist Party of Great Britain; however the idea never materialised and ended with Lord Redesdale meeting Claude Cockburn of the London Daily Worker, whom Jessica had persuaded to act as emissary. The outcome came about because the Communist Party felt that to share the island with the Redesdales was not likely to be of advantage to either party!

Unity Mitford, the youngest sister, was a friend of Hitler's during the Thirties and this led indirectly to her sad attempted suicide. This friendship also led to various rumours that U-boats landed spies on the coast of Inch Kenneth. This was never substantiated.

A view of Oban in the 1920s, with plenty of steam yachts and sailing ships, but before the Cathedral was built.

So this fascinating family with its divergent views and differing political outlook, were well-known Summer visitors to Mull and Inch Kenneth during the 1930s and 1940s.

Summary

Visitors today will find travelling so much easier than any of the travellers described in this collection, but they will still find just as much to fascinate and interest them, whether they call in at the Mull Museum in Tobermory for historical background or The Old Byre Centre in Dervaig, where displays of wildlife are on show.

Wildlife Safaris and sea trips to Staffa and the Treshnish Isles are there for those who want to explore further afield. Ferry services are available for those wanting to get to Kilchurn and to Coll and Tiree from Tobermory, and from Ulva Ferry one can go to Ulva or Staffa. Boats, coaches and passenger ferries connect from Oban via Craignure and Fionnphort with Iona.

There are castles and gardens to visit as well as many craft centres for those who want to take back a souvenir. The children whom Wordsworth criticised in 1833, would no doubt be amazed at the choice available today, although their humble sea-worn pebbles are still collected by visitors, who may also find the more valuable and exciting amethysts if they search diligently amongst the rocks.

Painters, fishermen, naturalists, botanists and geologists will all find plenty to interest them, for within the small area of these islands are many aspects of wildlife which are becoming scarce in other parts of the United Kingdom. These unspoilt areas are a joy to many who seek peace and quiet. Changes in the landscape are inevitably taking place, as the number of visitors increases and the requirements of these twentieth century travellers becomes more demanding, but the local interest, care and concern in preserving what is such a unique environment should mean that any change is not to the detriment of this sometimes very 'fragile' landscape.